The Beagle

Diane Morgan

The Beagle

Project Team
Editor: Stephanie Fornino
Copy Editor: Carl Schutt
Design: Mary Ann Kahn
Series Design: Mada Design
Series Originator: Dominique DeVito

T.F.H. Publications
President/CEO: Glen S. Axelrod
Executive Vice President: Mark E. Johnson
Publisher: Christopher T. Reggio
Production Manager: Kathy Bontz

T.F.H. Publications, Inc.
One TFH Plaza
Third and Union Avenues
Neptune City, NJ 07753

Printed and bound in China
06 07 08 09   3 5 7 9 8 6 4

Library of Congress Cataloging-in-Publication Data
Morgan, Diane, 1947- The beagle / Diane Morgan.
p. cm.
Includes index.
ISBN 0-7938-3627-1 (alk. paper)
1. Beagle (Dog breed) I. Title.
SF429.B3M653 2005
636.753'7--dc22
2005008464

This book has been published with the intent to provide accurate and authoritative information in regard to the subject matter within. While every precaution has been taken in preparation of this book, the author and publisher expressly disclaim responsibility for any errors, omissions, or adverse effects arising from the use or application of the information contained herein. The techniques and suggestions are used at the reader's discretion and are not to be considered a substitute for veterinary care. If you suspect a medical problem, consult your veterinarian.

The Leader In Responsible Animal Care For Over 50 Years!™
www.tfhpublications.com

TABLE OF CONTENTS

HISTORY 1
OF THE BEAGLE

Collies have Lassie, and German Shepherd Dogs have Rin Tin Tin—but Beagles have Snoopy! In fact, it took the great cartoonist Charles M. Schulz (1922-2000) and his immortal Beagle to show the world what Beaglers knew all along—that here is no ordinary Rover. And in case you're thinking that Snoopy is just a cartoon dog, you should think again. Snoopy is not only an American icon, but he is the very essence of Beagles. Debuting on October 2, 1950, Snoopy is a dog who dreams great dreams. At the time Snoopy made his entrance into the world, the Beagle was the number two dog in American Kennel Club registrations. Since then, the Beagle has never ranked lower than nine, and between 1953 and 1959, the Beagle was America's most popular dog.

Snoopy may be the all-American dog, the possessor of our dreams and secret soul mate, but he didn't arrive by accident. The advent of the Beagle onto the world stage was a notable and carefully planned event—at least sort of.

Beagles belong to a special class of dogs called hounds, dogs who are bred to chase their quarry to ground. Hounds come in two basic varieties: scenthounds like Beagles, Bassets, and Bloodhounds, and sighthounds like Greyhounds, Salukis, and Afghans. Both types of hounds are very nice, of course, but scenthounds tend to be more down to earth, in more ways than one. In the United States, Beagles are classified into two sizes: 13 and 15 inches, measuring from the top of the shoulder to the ground. Both varieties are equally charming and differ only in size. In the UK and most of the rest of the world, Beagles can range anywhere from 13 to 16 inches.

EARLY BEAGLES

Difficult as it may be to imagine, once there was a world without Beagles. This is probably a good thing, since the Beagle would have been no match for a Tyrannosaurus Rex. Evolutionarily speaking, of course, Beagles won out in the end, and I think it's no accident that Charles Darwin's exploring ship was named the *Beagle*!

Beagles belong to a special class of dogs called hounds.

The word "Beagle" itself may derive from the French word *begle*, which in turn comes from the medieval *begueule*, meaning "gape-throated." This was a derogatory term stemming from a Latin root for "gullet." It probably referred to the loud voice of the Beagle, although a rival derivation suggests that the throat, and hence the appetite of the dog, was small. (I'm not really sure about this—for a small dog, a Beagle can eat a lot!)

A completely different explanation of the name draws upon the ancient Gaelic tongue. In Gaelic, for instance, *beag* means "of little worth." The term may not mean that the dog himself was of little value, but rather that the game he pursued, rabbits and hares, was of less significance than deer, elk, or boar.

Python Pete and the Swamp Monsters

Beagles battle swamp monsters to this day. In the Florida Everglades, there is a growing problem with Burmese pythons who have been dumped there by their owners. These pythons can grow up to 14 feet long, by the way, and have been photographed engaged in battle with alligators. They also gobble up wading birds and deer. Everglades park officials have an answer: Python Pete. Python Pete is a young Beagle who is being trained in the delicate art of snake tracking. Once fully trained, he will sniff out the deadly constrictors and alert his handlers to their presence, although he has strict instructions not to attempt to tackle the monsters himself.

Merrie Proto-Beagles in Merrie Old England

The first dogs that we can reliably call "Beagles" came from England. The legendary King Arthur supposedly possessed a pack of white scenthounds vaguely resembling Beagles, but because the very existence of Arthur is questionable, his hounds can only be a rumor. Still, it's such an interesting thought that I'm not willing to throw away the idea that today's Beagles are the true-born descendants of those ancient and royal hounds.

We also know that when the Romans invaded England in 43 C.E., they brought along their small hounds, distant ancestors to the present-day Beagles. No one knows what became of them, but it's only reasonable to assume that they mixed with the native canine population, probably in a random way.

The Pocket Harrier

But let's move on to somewhat more relevant history. In 1066, William the Conqueror brought two types of hounds to England, of the types mentioned earlier: sighthounds who hunted by sight and scenthounds who hunted by nose. (The latter were called Talbot hounds.) The early aristocracy used both sorts of hounds for hunting.

The fourteenth century was an exciting time for Beagle breeders. (It seems that some of the earliest Beagles may even have been wirehaired!) One of their more ingenious

The first Beagles came from England, and legend states that King Arthur's dogs were the ancestors of contemporary Beagles.

Nivek Beagles, a kennel in the United Kingdom, can trace the noble ancestors of their Beagles back to 1705 in an unbroken line.

"products" was a close relation of the Beagle, a sort of toy hound standing only 5 to 9 inches high. This little Glove, or Pocket Harrier, as the dog was known, could be stuffed into a gauntlet or tucked neatly into a saddlebag or basket and then carried along on a hunt. Edward II (1307-1327) kept a pack of them. This dog was particularly noted for his elegant voice, and hence was given the name "singing Beagle."

Although faddish with the sporting set for a while, breeders finally caught on to the fact that Pocket Harriers weren't such a great idea after all, as they were too small to be of much practical use. Be that as it may, Queen Elizabeth I (1558-1603) and her grandfather, Henry VII (1485-1509), both had whole passels of them. They used to let them loose after the bigger dogs had already charged ahead. Eventually, however, these little dogs largely disappeared.

Full-Sized Beagles

Full-sized Beagles may have begun as foxhounds or harriers during the time of Henry VIII (1509-1547) and his daughter Elizabeth I, when fox hunting became popular among the rich. Before that time, royalty were given to chasing deer around in the woods, and the hound of choice was a great big creature called a "buckhound." Some people think that buckhounds were crossed with small rabbit hunting dogs to create foxhounds, and Beagles were subsequently developed from that group. It is also possible that, as is sometimes claimed, terrier blood was introduced to reduce the size of the larger hounds.

Other authorities, however, deny that Beagles were "bred down" from foxhounds or buckhounds and point out that Beagle-like dogs could be found long before fox

Full-sized Beagles may have begun as foxhounds or harriers during the reign of King Henry VIII.

hunting became a royal pastime. They suggest that foxhounds may have been "bred up" from Beagles rather than the other way around. (Terriers and spaniels have been implicated in both the "bred up" and "bred down" theories.) The truth will probably never be known; certainly, the surviving paintings upon which most of the "evidence" is based have more charm than breed accuracy.

For a while, Beagles were actually in danger of becoming extinct, because fox hunting began to replace rabbit hunting among the sporting set. These folks preferred using true foxhounds, as they were bigger and faster, and Beagle numbers declined dangerously. Beagles survived only because rabbit hunting was still important among small-time farmers in southern England and Wales. They hunted not so much for sport but to supplement their diet.

At any rate, by the mid 1700s, two Beagle-type dogs were in existence: One was the so-called Southern Hound, a large, deep-voiced, long-eared animal (possibly resembling today's Basset Hound, although only loosely related to him). This dog may have been descended from the white Talbot Hound, one of the hounds brought over with William the Conqueror. The other Beagle-type dog was the quicker, hard-running North Country Beagle, whose voice had a higher pitched, "yappier" tone. Some researchers claim that there was yet a third Beagle type, one even smaller than the North Country Beagle. This was an economical hunting companion—a charming, playful creature with a small appetite who was apparently easily distracted and unreliable. Probably all three types contributed to the development of the modern Beagle.

THE MODERN BEAGLE

The Modern Beagle in the UK

The Kennel Club of the United Kingdom recognized the Beagle in 1873. Eight years later, the Association of Masters of Harriers and Beagles was formed. (The Harrier is a foxhunting dog midway in size between a foxhound and a Beagle.) In England, the Beagle Club was formed in 1890 "to promote the breeding of Beagles for show and sporting purposes," while the Association of Masters of Harriers and Beagles maintained strictly an interest in the hunting aspect of the breed. In 1895, the Beagle Club published a "Standard of Points" that is very similar to today's Kennel Club breed standard, and in 1897, the Beagle Club sponsored its first show.

World War I was devastating to dog breeding in general—it was hard enough even to get enough food for people. Practically all show breeding was abandoned, and the sport of dog showing didn't get going again until the 1920s. Even then, however, few Beagles were in existence. The rebirth of Beagles in England was largely due to a woman named Nina Elms, who had a passion not only for Beagles, but also for Bassets and Bloodhounds. She called her kennel Reynalton, and it is said that she showed up at the famous Crufts Dog show with 60 dogs entered among the three breeds.

Things turned bad again for Beagles with the onset of World War II, and in 1945, only one new Beagle was registered with the Kennel Club. But as always, the Beagle survived, largely because working hunters in all parts of the country knew a good breed when they saw one, and they kept breeding their Beagles, even if most of them were not registered.

The Modern Beagle in America

We can credit the creation of today's American Beagle primarily to an Essex County (England) clergyman in the mid 1800s. This fellow, who bore the delightful name of Parson Phillip Honeywood, assembled the first pack of sporting Beagles. He got his Beagles by mixing up some of his original stock with Otterhounds and Bloodhounds. This sounds like a strange combination, but it worked. Honeywood and his cronies formed a little club of sorts called the Merry Beaglers of the Meadows, and they began to amuse themselves by chasing rabbits and hares all over the countryside. The story goes that the good Parson's hounds, while clever hunters, were not all that much to look at. However, a fellow Englishman, Thomas Johnson, remedied

Historical accounts of what early Beagles may have looked like differ over whether the modern version is leggier and rangier than his earlier counterpart.

the situation by producing a pack of hounds who were as handsome as they were good hunters.

It's a matter of controversy as to what exactly these early Beagles looked like. Some contend they were leggier and rangier than modern examples, while others claim just the opposite. Judging from the contemporary paintings, whose accuracy, as I pointed out earlier, may be historically suspect, both kinds of Beagles were present. It's certainly safe to say that what we now know as the "Beagle type" had not yet been fixed, and breeders consulted their own preferences to a larger degree than is true today, now that quality Beagles must adhere to a breed standard. In the United States, the early Beagle was a mostly white hound, bearing only a few dark or tan markings. This dog was an excellent hunter, but according to the American Kennel Club's official history, not much to look at. Even the show Beagles were rangier than the approved British sort. They were often pied or mottled, and ranged in size from a toy size to 16 inches in height as the British standard allowed.

In the early days, the American Beagle resembled a cross between a badly bred Dachshund and an unusual-looking Basset Hound. To improve the dog's appearance, several American breeders imported some British stock. One of these breeders was General Richard Rowett of Carlinville, Illinois (an immigrant from England originally), aided by Norman Elmore of Newark, New Jersey. Around 1876, Rowett imported some northern English Beagles (source unknown), including the infamous Rosey and Dolly, and from them developed a line of Beagles known as "Kerry Beagles."

Rowett's dogs were the first dual-purpose Beagles, being of high show quality and strong hunting ability. The Rowett strain was later continued by Pottinger Dorsey and Staley Doub of Maryland, who bred dogs noted for their excellent and uniform type, as well as for their powerful hunting ability.

In 1896, James Kernochan of Rhode Island (Hempstead Beagles) imported some hunting Beagles from the famous Royal Rock Beagle Pack of England. These animals possessed the desirable head and neck qualities that were lacking in the American types. The third breeder, also from Rhode Island, was a man known to history only as Mr. Arnold of Providence. Mr. Arnold apparently had the grave

Rowett apparently had a gift for breeding good animals. He also bred the 15th winner of the Kentucky Derby, a horse named Spokane. In addition, he was a minor hero of the Civil War, having participated in the bloody battle of Allatoona (1864).

In the United States, early Beagles were mostly white hounds with a few dark or tan markings; today's version sports a wider variety of color.

misfortune of losing his first name somewhere, but luckily he managed to hang on to most of his Beagles. He and Kernochan were great fans of field trialing, and they organized the first such Beagle events in America.

In 1888, two years before a similar organization formed in England, the National Beagle Club was formed in the United States with its stated objective being to hold field trials to improve hunting ability as well as conformation. Its purpose was to set the standard and work for the betterment of this popular hunting dog. When the National Beagle Club applied for admission to the American Kennel Club as a specialty club, though, it was turned down because the American-English Beagle Club (the first Beagle specialty club, founded in 1884), or American Beagle Club as it was also known, refused to sanction its admission.

Undaunted, the new club continued with its plans and eventually merged with the American Beagle Club. The combined club was called the National Beagle Club of America, or NBC. The standard was revised in 1900 to put more emphasis on running gear (the front and back legs and feet).

The first National Beagle Club field trial was originally held in New Hampshire in 1890. The first National Beagle Club Specialty Show was held in 1891. For quite a while in the United States, field trials were emphasized at the expense of conformation. Trials became bigger and more frequent, and eventually the Beagle Advisory Commission of the American Kennel Club was formed in 1936 to oversee field trials. Even today, the people who serve on this committee are Beaglers from different parts of the country who are active in the sport and who are selected by their peers. They serve with no pay.

Breeders near Philadelphia established the first American Beagle specialty club in 1884, the same year that the American Kennel Club was founded. (The first Beagle registered with the American Kennel Club, in 1885, was a dog named Blunder.) The new club worked hard to develop a single standard for their breed. Up to that time, as I mentioned, Beagles ranged widely in size and appearance. But with care and attention, a stable American Beagle type emerged, one similar to but somewhat larger and perhaps more "balanced" than the British version.

Probably the most famous American Beagles were Lyndon Johnson's Him and Her. One of the great early show Beagles was Stoke Pace Sapper, originally from England. Sapper, as he was called, arrived in America in 1915 and quickly made his influence felt throughout the Beagle community in America. (He was sold once for $250, a remarkable sum in those days.) Sapper sired winning show dogs up to the time of his death at 12 years of age in 1923, including 22 bench champions, multiple field champions, and even two dual champions.

Today, the Beagle remains one of America's most beloved canine companions. His unrelenting popularity, in fact, is a testament to his stable temperament and versatility in the home, field, and show ring.

The American Kennel Club (AKC), founded in 1884, is the most influential dog club in the United States. The AKC is a "club of clubs," meaning that its members are other kennel clubs, not individual people. The AKC registers purebred dogs, supervises dog shows, and is concerned with all dog-related matters, including public education and legislation. It collects and publishes the official standards for all of its recognized breeds. The United Kingdom version of the AKC is called the Kennel Club. However, the Kennel Club's members are individual persons. The membership of the Kennel Club is restricted to a maximum of 1,500 UK members in addition to 50 overseas members and a small number of honorary life members. The Kennel Club promotes responsible dog ownership and works on important issues like canine health and welfare.

The Beagle is one of America's most beloved canine companions.

CHARACTERISTICS

O F   T H E   B E A G L E

Welcome to the world of the beautiful and beguiling Beagle! Currently, Beagles rank fourth in the number of AKC registrations, with 44,555 registered in 2004; however, this is a deceptive figure. Many Beagles, even many great Beagles, are not AKC registered. Many hunters and others who work their Beagles on a regular basis but do not show their dogs don't bother with AKC registration. (This is also because other registrations exist for them.) There are a lot more Beagles out there than is apparent from some official statistics!

There are many good reasons for the Beagle's tremendous, unremitting popularity. For one thing, they love you for you and not your possessions. They don't care if you've gotten a trifle slow or creaky (although they don't excuse slowness if it makes dinner five minutes late). They don't mind if you've gained a bit of weight recently or if you're having a bad hair day. Beagles are far more discerning than that, and so are you if this is your chosen breed. Beagles take a lot of work and a lot of love, but they give more than they take: happy days, snuggly nights, and warm memories. This insanely optimistic dog has a tail that wags even when he's sleeping. You will never, ever be sorry you shared your life with this most engaging of dogs.

THE JOYS OF BEAGLING

Beagles are versatile animals who fit happily in most households. They are a convenient size, for one thing, neither so large that they take up the entire couch nor so small that you can't find them in the living room. With moderate care and a great deal of love, the Beagle will take his natural place as a very special member of the family.

Exercise Requirements

Like most dogs with a hunting background, Beagles need plenty of vigorous exercise, but a secure backyard and a dedicated owner can easily provide a sufficient amount. These dogs love to be outdoors and off on exciting adventures with you, but they just as easily snuggle up in your lap and snooze away the long winter evenings by the fireside.

Beagles need a good deal of exercise to keep fit, but they also have a lazy streak. You can habituate your Beagle to lying around all day, but it won't be good for him. Beagles tend not to

Much of the popularity of the Beagle is due to his optimistic and engaging personality.

self-exercise, though, so you'll have to be prepared for long hikes a couple of times a week to keep him healthy. I have also found that smaller Beagles tend to be more active than larger ones.

Watchdog

Beagles are superb watchdogs. Alert and observant, they will bark noisily at the first sign of a trespasser, yet their cheerful, amiable dispositions make them entirely safe as pets.

Sociability

Beagles need plenty of exercise to keep them fit.

Because Beagles are pack oriented, they are not "one-person" dogs. Beagles like everyone in the family (and

visitors, too). You don't have to worry about a Beagle sulking or going off his feed if his favorite person can't be with him every moment of the week.

Although most breeds of dogs can *learn* to be sociable around children, children and Beagles are a natural team. Beagles are outgoing and tolerant dogs, and as long as they are not frightened or abused, they take naturally to children.

Small enough to be disarming, energetic enough to play for hours, and friendly enough to win any congeniality contest, I would rank the Beagle as the number-one breed in the world to get along with kids. Of course, there can be exceptions, and some Beagles are too shy to be ideal playmates. Beagles are not retrievers, however, and they don't usually care for games like fetch. Nor are they to be trusted off-lead away from your home, no matter how earnestly your child may insist he or she will watch the dog. Beagles can outsmart children and can easily give them the slip when on the trail of an intriguing smell.

Of course, it's your job to teach your kids how to deal with a dog. Even young children can learn how to gently

Young Beagles should be exercised gently, because overexercise can damage growing bones and joints.

brush the dog, and older ones can help you walk him. By the time a child is seven or eight years old, she can feed the dog—but only if you supervise. And preteens and older kids can learn a lot by going to puppy kindergarten with you!

All children need to be taught how to respect the dog. This means leaving him alone when he's eating or sleeping or when he indicates he has had enough by walking away. It means not overwhelming the puppy with overzealous petting, no hugging or kissing (which can seem

Beagles are outgoing and tolerant dogs who take naturally to children.

frightening to a young dog), and no screaming or chasing.

Beagles also socialize well with other pets, especially if raised with them. They like cats and other dogs (especially other Beagles). If they have a fault in this area, it's that they might be just a little *too* interested in Hopalong, the pet rabbit. That, of course, is owing to their heritage, because Beagles were developed primarily as a hunting breed. Observe your Beagle carefully with smaller pets before you leave them alone together.

Possessiveness

Some Beagles can be very possessive of their food, and you should teach children to leave a dining dog strictly alone. Beagles eat pretty fast, so this shouldn't be too much of a hardship, even for the most impatient child. In other respects, Beagles are quite willing to share. This breed has extremely few problems related to temperament if you exclude stubbornness.

Barking

No doubt about it, Beagles can bark rings around most other breeds. It's part of their inherited makeup, as hunting Beagles signal a find by "baying." Your Beagle will let you know about all visitors, including visiting cats. If neglected, that can turn to mournful howling. However, they are not in general "nuisance barkers," that is, barking for no reason, although you might not always be aware of the cause. (For more information on problem barking, see Chapter 6.)

Hardiness

Beagles are tough dogs who tolerate both heat and cold very well. This doesn't mean they should be left outside, however, because they do not tolerate being left alone. It does mean they can join you for romps in all seasons and all weathers.

Trainability

Beagles generally rank rather low on most trainability lists, but that's because people are not training them to do things that Beagles find interesting. Beagles are extremely intelligent dogs who are smart enough to do what interests them rather than following a bunch of commands.

However, if you are interested in a supremely good rabbit hunting companion, the Beagle is your dog. It's what they were bred for and where they excel. These are the premier rabbit hunting dogs in all the world, and if you want to see your dog really shine, you might consider this sport.

Of course, Beagles can and should be taught basic good manners, and with extreme patience, you can enter into formal obedience with your dog. Realistic expectations from the beginning will make for a happy partnership.

Grooming Requirements

Beagles are easy to groom, even though their hair is technically medium in length, not short. However, they are shedders, as are most double-coated dogs. Beagles shed moderately throughout the year, but you can lessen the effects by frequently and thoroughly brushing them.

Although Beagles can tolerate both hot and cold weather, they should never be left outside.

Health Problems

Beagles are generally healthy dogs, although like every other breed, certain problems are rather common. Skin problems, cancer, eye problems, and neurological disorders can plague the breed, although Beagles are certainly no less healthy than most other contemporary purebred dogs.

Longevity

As a bonus, Beagles live a very long time, for dogs. They attain an average age of 15; generations of Irish Wolfhounds or Newfoundlands can pass through your life during that time. Some Beagles even reach the age of 20!

THE BEAGLE BREED STANDARD

A breed standard is a written picture of the ideal dog. Because it refers to the ultimate dog, most pet Beagles don't

Canine Sniffing Machines

Beagles are not only cute and charming, but they are also smart and useful working dogs. One Beagle named Peaches earned her living by sniffing out termites for a firm in Scranton, Pennsylvania. Her fame spread far and wide until she was issued a challenge: Could Peaches outsniff professional human pest inspectors with fancy termite detectors? Peaches was pitted against the competition at a church with known termite problems in State College, Pennsylvania. Presiding over the affair was Dr. Robert Snetsinger, a professor of entomology. Everyone stood by nervously as Peaches was given her cue: "Termites!" Instantly, Peaches went into "attack" mode, trembling all over. She immediately discovered every known termite infestation, plus 12 other sites unknown to the judges. As a bonus, she found some colonies of carpenter ants. The human pest inspectors were still lugging their equipment around the building by the time Peaches had completed her assignment. Her reward? Three chili dogs at a local fast food place.

meet every criterion perfectly. In fact, not even a Westminster Best of Breed Beagle is perfect. Still, it is always interesting to examine the standard to see how well our own dogs compare with the ideal picture. If he doesn't measure up technically, that okay. He's still the best dog in the world!

All dog breeds recognized by the American Kennel Club (US) or Kennel Club (UK) must conform to a breed standard developed by the national club of that breed. Each breed club keeps the studbook for its breed and works hard to make sure that its show dogs approach the written standard. The standard is there for comparison purposes. Beagles should look like Beagles and not like Dachshunds or Basset Hounds, which is what might happen if people were left to create their own individual standards.

Beagles Come in Two Sizes

The first thing to note is that for competition purposes in the United States, Beagles come in two varieties based on size. The smaller Beagle cannot exceed 13 inches at the withers (top of the shoulder), while the larger cannot exceed 15 inches at the withers for bench competition or field trials. Two inches may not seem like much, but when you're a little dog, every inch counts. Most other countries, however, including the UK, recognize the correct size for Beagles as anywhere between 13 and 16 inches, without a division into

All dog breeds recognized by the AKC or KC must conform to a breed standard, a written ideal picture of the dog.

two standard sizes. Smaller Beagles generally weigh less than 20 pounds, and the larger ones may weigh up to about 30 pounds. If your Beagle is 15 inches, he really shouldn't weigh more than this; if he does, he is probably overweight, a huge problem among Beagles. In today's world, the 15-inch Beagle is the more usual size, perhaps because of better nutrition and outcrossing among Beagle breeders (which means breeding away from one's own line). Nowadays, most Beagle kennels try to breed and compete with just one height category for the sake of consistency within their breeding programs. However, there are no guarantees. Beagles maturing to different heights can and do occur in the same litter, so if you get a puppy, you'll just have to wait and see how big he grows.

Different Job, Different Beagle?

In the early days, most Beagles were dual purpose dogs who competed with equal aplomb in conformation and field work or hunting. Indeed, the Beagle foundation dogs in the United States were imported from the best British hunting packs. Things are different in these days of specialization, however. For better or for worse, Beagles come in different "types," each having a specific function. (The Beagle standards in the US and UK make no mention of this, but everyone in Beagles knows it's true.) There are conformation or bench Beagles (these are the ones you see in the show ring), but they are not as adept at field-work as other types. There are also "brace" Beagles used in field trials. These dogs have superior noses, but they move so slowly that many hunters prefer to use dogs of their own breeding. Fortunately, there's room for all kinds of Beagles and all kinds of owners in the Beagle world.

While most people have heard of the American Kennel Club (AKC), the United States is home to another highly respected but lesser known club—the United Kennel Club (UKC), which was created in 1898. This club is performance-oriented, although it also has conformation shows. The heart of the club however, is its collection of events: agility, obedience, hunting tests, retriever trials, and weight pulls. The UKC recognizes 308 dog breeds, far more than the AKC, including, for example, six kinds of coonhounds alone. It licenses 10,000 events a year, mostly hunting and working trials. The UKC's conformation shows are smaller and much more casual than AKC affairs. It divides breeds into eight groups (the AKC has seven): Companion, Guardian, Gun, Herding, Northern, Sighthounds and Pariahs, Scenthounds, and Terriers.

Beagles bred for conformation and Beagles bred for field work or hunting may have very different temperaments.

Nearly any type of Beagle can make a great pet, although the personality of conformation types may be best suited for people who don't plan on hunting with their dogs. Field trial and hunting Beagles are more intense, single-minded dogs, but they too can fit in perfectly with the right household. Dogs from these lines are often more available as well, because many breeders who primarily breed for hunting ability look for good pet homes in which to place Beagles who don't "cut it" in the field.

Interpreting the Standards

The following description of the Beagle is based on interpretations of both the American Kennel Club and Kennel Club's breed standards. (To read both breed standards in their entirety, refer to the appendix.)

Head

The earliest AKC standard (1884) paid more attention to the head than to almost anything else, awarding it 35 out of a possible 100 total points (for show judging purposes). That number has been lowered today to 25 percent of the total points in favor of giving more points to the running gear and body.

The UK standard states that the Beagle's head should be powerful without sign of coarseness, and it should be free from frown and wrinkle.

Skull

A Beagle needs a good nose, and a good nose needs a good head. The British standard remarks that the skull is finer in the bitch than in the male dog. Although the American standard makes no specific mention of a difference between sexes, it is generally acknowledged that male dogs

The earliest UK standard paid more attention to the head than to anything else.

should look like male dogs, and female dogs should look like female dogs.

Ears

The American Kennel Club ear requirement, which is very similar to that of the Kennel Club, calls for the Beagle's ears to be set moderately low, long, fine in texture, fairly broad, and with an almost entire absence of erectile power. Even though the standard calls for this absence of erectile power, in point of fact, the Beagle can raise his ears to some extent when interested.

The Beagle's ears should be set moderately low and long, with a fine texture.

Eyes

Beagles can manage to look pleading even when you are not chomping down on a hamburger in front of them. They can also look very merry, a word that is mentioned in the British standard but not in the American standard. In any case, sharp "terrier-like" eyes or protruding eyes are a definite fault in Beagles. The AKC standard says they should

Most Beagles are slightly "off square," meaning they are just a bit longer than they are high.

be large, while the KC standard maintains that they should be fairly large. Thankfully, no one has appended an actual measurement requirement.

Muzzle

According to the AKC standard, a sharp, "snipy" muzzle is a defect, as is a muzzle that is long or very short. The British standard says that a black nose is preferable, while the American standard doesn't seem to have an opinion on the matter.

Jaws

In both the AKC and KC standards, the jaws should meet without being undershot or overshot. It is generally considered that the best bite is a "scissors" bite, where the upper teeth slightly overlap the lower ones. Although a level bite (one in which the upper and lower teeth meet evenly) is also acceptable in the AKC standard, this can cause too much wear on the teeth.

Neck and Throat

Beagles should not have a thick, ugly neck or a throat with the folds of skin (dewlaps) characteristic of a Basset Hound. Dogs with heavy throats like this are called, logically enough, "throaty." The British standard draws specific attention to a "slightly arched" neck, which gives elegance to the carriage. In the show ring, Beagles and other scenthounds are required to zip around the ring with their heads head high. (The handlers attach the leashes in such a way that they essentially force this position.) In the real world, of course, the Beagle spends a lot of time sniffing the earth, and even when he moves forward quickly, tends to keep his head forward rather than high.

Shoulders and Chest

It is important that the Beagle's shoulders not be straight and upright, because this interferes with good movement. A disproportionately broad chest also interferes with free striding.

Back, Loin, and Ribs

You don't want to see a Beagle with a swayed back or one who is humped or roached, as they say in dog show language. The side view should reveal a straight back or topline, with a slight arch over the loin. The American standard doesn't actually mention a straight topline, but everyone knows it should be there, and in fact, most good Beagles have an excellent topline. Flat ribs are a defect.

Forelegs and Feet

According to the AKC standard, the forelegs should be straight, with short, straight pasterns. (The pastern is the area between the front carpus, or "knee," and the feet.) The legs

should be substantial, with plenty of bone. Beagles are not delicate toy Poodles. The front legs should be strong looking and straight; they should parallel the hind legs.

The Kennel Club standard adds that the feet should be tight and firm, with short nails.

A Beagle who doesn't exactly measure up to a breed standard can still make a terrific pet.

Hips, Thighs, Hind Legs, and Feet

Hips and thighs should be strong and well muscled, giving abundance or propelling power. Stifles should be strong and well let down, and the hocks should be firm, symmetrical, and moderately bent. The feet should be close and firm. Viewed from the back, the hocks shouldn't be turned into each other, a condition called "cowhocks." The feet should be tight and catlike, not open or spreading.

Tail

The AKC standard stipulates that the tail must be set moderately high and carried gaily. It should have a slight curve, be short compared to the size of the dog, and have "brush." That brush is very important! It is assumed that brush on the tail helps protect it from injury, although I am not sure this is true. It can also get caught in stickers more easily. However, some show people trim this brush, although they shouldn't. (The standard calls for a generally natural-looking dog, and a somewhat brushy tail is really a hallmark of the breed.) Show Beagles in the United States often carry their tails higher than is acceptable in the UK, where people

The British standard stipulates that the Beagle's tail should have a white tip.

prefer the tail to be carried at a "five minutes past the hour" angle. In any case, it should be carried up; a lowered or tucked-in tail indicates fear and misery.

Although the American standard doesn't actually say this, it's generally conceded that the tail should have a white tip on it. This supposedly makes it easier for hunters to find their dogs in the bush; the tail acts as a flag or signal. The British standard makes it a requirement that the tail (or "stern" as it is phrased) must be tipped white. The tail should be strong and tapered,

Gait

The UK standard says that the Beagle's stride should be "free, long reaching in front and straight without high action; hind legs showing drive." The AKC standard does not mention gait.

Coat

The Beagle's coat should be dense and shiny and not feel soft to the touch. The Beagle is a hunting dog whose coat should be able to repel stickers and water. The British standard specifically says that the coat should be waterproof.

Color

The AKC standard states that the Beagle can be any true hound color. Beagles come in an amazing variety of colors, and most are two or three different colors. The National

Beagle Club of America assumes that "hound colors" include all shades and combinations of white (or cream), black, tan/lemon/red, brown/liver, blue/gray, and the colors of the hare ("hare pied") or badger ("badger pied"). Almost all Beagles also have white on their bodies, which shows up in the so-called "Irish spotting" pattern on the face, neck, legs, and tail tip. Other Beagles have a solid tan face. So-called "open marked" or "piebald hounds" have more white in the background. That's okay, too.

Most Beagles are what we call "tricolor." Tricolor dogs have a black saddle with a white chest and underbelly. Tricolor dogs often have brown or tan faces. However, there are also varieties of tricolor dogs: shaded tris, faded tris, chocolate tris, blue tris, and classic tris! The classic tricolor, which is a perennial favorite, has very clear-cut markings. One should note that many future tricolor puppies are born black and white; the tan comes in later. Beagles who are born black and white and remain black and white are extremely rare. Most Beagles have some white on them, but an all-white Beagle is extremely rare, although the coloring is perfectly permissible. (A rare color does not necessarily mean a desirable color, though. Most people just don't want an all-white Beagle.) Blue occurs as a dilute of the tricolor gene but can be changed in color *depth* by the same modifier genes that control the various shades of red and white. Many dilutes have lighter colored eyes than the "purer" colors; some, in fact, have almost yellow eyes. Some also have a slate

In the world of showing, it's well known that color can create an optical illusion, revealing or masking good or bad qualities. In fact, color can make one side of the dog appear different from another, and it can also cause the dog to appear less symmetrical than he really is.

Tricolored Beagles often have brown or tan faces.

In general, a Beagle should appear sturdy, compact, and well balanced.

blue nose. Other Beagles even have ticking or freckles, rather like a German Shorthaired Pointer. This pattern is known as mottled.

Beagles can come in red and white as well. In Beagledom, red can be anything from light tan to very dark brown. There is also a lemon color, a pale unearthly shade. Lemon puppies are born all white. Sometimes you'll also hear the term "patch Beagle," a phrase that refers to both lemon and white and red and white Beagles. It can also be used to refer to mostly white dogs with a big tricolored spot. Show ring judges seem to have developed a taste for red and white Beagles recently (a trend I have also noted in Bassets), but the standard doesn't prefer one color above another.

The British standard does not allow liver color in Beagles, although it allows all "hound colors." Being hounds, you'll find Beagles with freckling (officially called ticking), grizzling, mottling, and other interesting varieties. All are acceptable. Stripes and polka dots are another matter, of course. In general, dark or tricolored Beagles seem to have fewer skin problems than those of lighter coloration. Interestingly enough, a litter of puppies may well contain puppies with lots of different colors!

General Appearance

The AKC standard describes the Beagle's general appearance as "a miniature Foxhound, solid and big for his inches, with the wear-and-tear look of a hound that can last in the chase and follow his quarry to the death." Following one's quarry to the death is all very well in its place, I suppose, although the idea may make some (like me) a bit squeamish! This language derives directly from the original 1884 standard. The British standard describes the Beagle's general appearance as sturdy, compact, and conveying the impression of quality without coarseness, with no mention of following one's quarry to the death.

In general, a Beagle should be well balanced, meaning that his front and hind parts should look as if they belong to the same dog. The reason is not simply a matter of aesthetics, but of practicality as well. An unbalanced dog is not the sure, tireless runner that a Beagle must be to be worthy of the name.

Temperament

The American standard does not refer to temperament. The British standard is more forthright in discussing the ideal: "Amiable and alert, showing no aggression or timidity." The British standard also describes the Beagle as "a merry hound whose essential function is to hunt, primarily hare, by following a scent. Bold, with great activity, stamina and determination. Alert, intelligent, and of even temperament." It is important for Beagles to possess what we call a "pack mentality," because age-old Beagle tradition requires them to hunt in packs. And indeed, most Beagles are the most sociable creatures imaginable, both with humans and with other dogs. This is one of their greatest charms.

That does not mean that every Beagle has a perfect temperament. Some are shy, and most are stubborn. However, it may comfort you to know that over the years, Beagles have probably become more biddable than their ancestors, undoubtedly because most now go to homes as pets. (Lines of hunting Beagles, on the other hand, retain their "let's do it my way" attitude.) This does not mean that you can trust your Beagle to come to you when he is off lead. Even if your Beagle has never smelled a rabbit before in his life, rest assured that the first day you let him off lead will be the day he smells a rabbit and takes off. In fact, while Beagles are quite willing to please you, they cannot or will not reliably return to you if they have caught a scent that interests them.

YOUR BEAGLE'S SENSES

Understanding your Beagle means understanding the way he experiences the world. He does this through his senses of smell, sight, hearing, touch, and taste.

Smell

Your Beagle may go blind, deaf, or both, but as long as he can smell, he'll be pretty satisfied with life. Not only does your dog have a lot of olfactory receptors lining the mucous

membranes of his nose (about 40 times more than we have), but he also has a special mass of tissue called the vomeronasal organ embedded in the hard palate that appears to be useful for sexual signals. In addition, dogs have a much larger (proportionally) olfactory lobe in the brain than we do. In fact, it's been estimated that a dog's sense of smell is 1,000 times better than ours. Dogs smell so well that they can detect the individual components that go into the makeup of any odor. You may smell pumpkin pie, for example, but your dog smells sugar, eggs, graham crackers, and so on. Some intriguing studies have been performed to investigate a dog's ability to "smell out" skin cancer, breast cancer, and bladder cancer in people.

Sight

Like most predators, dogs have forward-facing eyes (as opposed to the sideways-positioned eyes of most prey animals). This placement gives them depth perception, although some peripheral vision is sacrificed. Still, dogs have much wider peripheral vision than we do—about 240 degrees compared to about 180 degrees in people. Dogs are also better than humans at perceiving moving objects.

Despite the myth that dogs only see in black and white, they do see some colors like blue, yellow, and shades of gray. In fact, they can detect differences in blue better than people. Red and green are a mystery to them, however.

In terms of night vision, dogs far outpace us, partly because their eyes contain a large number of rod photoreceptors rather than color-perceiving cones. Dogs also have a special layer of tissue (the tapetum lucidum) behind the retina that helps gather light and reflect it back to the retina a second time. That's what causes a dog's green "eyeshine."

Hearing

Dogs have great ears—even Beagles, whose ears are droopy and have only limited mobility. Studies have not shown that prick-eared breeds hear better than lop-eared dogs like Beagles. Dogs are adapted to hear sounds important to them, like the sound of a mouse squeaking underground or that of a refrigerator opening ever so softly. Your Beagle can also hear much higher pitched sounds than we can.

Touch

Like humans, dogs have several different methods of processing "touch." They have mechanoreceptors that work to detect pressure, nociceptors that signal pain, and thermoceptors that tell them about heat and cold. Dogs can also use their whiskers, which are modified hairs, to absorb information about the world that surrounds them. (The whiskers' roots are surrounded by sinuses that contain nerve endings.)

Taste

You may notice that your Beagle eats everything rather indiscriminately. Partly this is what it means to be a dog. Dogs have far fewer taste buds than people, and what they do have are located farther back in the oral cavity—with a few even heading down the throat. In other words, your Beagle tastes foods as he swallows them, not before. In fact, even compared with other dogs, Beagles are pretty indiscriminate in their tasting habits. Dog food companies won't even use Beagles in their taste tests because these dogs don't care if they are eating gourmet food or garbage.

Beagles are excellent dogs in every way. If you want a dog with the elegance of an Irish Setter, the brains of a Border Collie, the trainability of a Golden Retriever, and the feisty temperament of a terrier, go ahead and get one of those dogs. But if you want a charming, lively, happy-go-lucky companion to share your life, make you smile, and nourish your spirit, then the Beagle is really the only sensible choice. Beagles are blessed with the best temperaments in the canine world, the kindest hearts, and the friendliest faces. Who could ask for more?

3 PREPARING

FOR YOUR BEAGLE

While owning a Beagle can be a fantastic experience, things usually go more smoothly if you have some warning that a Beagle is coming into your life so that you can prepare. And while this may not mean you have to read-just your stock portfolio, you may have to move some furniture, change your sleeping schedule, and send the kids off to boarding school. I am just kidding, of course. You can usually keep the furniture where it is.

It is important to realize that dogs do require a lot of care and time. Many dogs are purchased on a whim by people who really have neither the time, energy, nor inclination to look after them. As a result, the dogs don't have their needs met. This chapter will help you select the perfect Beagle for you and your family, as well as prepare for his arrival in your home.

FINDING A BEAGLE

Beagles are easy to find, but be careful. Choosing a Beagle is not like picking up a quart of milk at the grocery store. A dog is not a disposable commodity—a dog is for keeps! Your Beagle will be your companion, snuggle buddy, and best friend for many years to come. Although all Beagles may be equally good, not all are equally good for you. You'll need to consult your own needs and preferences before choosing the dog who will become your companion. Choose wisely.

Incredible as it may seem, not everyone should own a dog, let alone a super dog like a Beagle. Adding a Beagle to your family is like acquiring a new child. He is a friend who will be with you as long as he lives. If this is your first dog or your first Beagle, you will have to rely on others to help you make the best choice about your new pet. This may be a breeder, veterinarian, knowledgeable friend, or responsible rescue. You don't have to do it alone, and you shouldn't.

Steel yourself; buy with your head as well as your heart. Some experts recommend visiting at least three different places before you purchase your Beagle. To prevent impulse buying, do not bring your

Choose wisely when considering what Beagle is best for you and your family.

checkbook on your first visit. One look in those sweet brown eyes and it will all be over. Make yourself go home, rethink your decision, and if you're *sure*, then go back and bring home (or reserve) your puppy. Of course, if you've traveled 500 miles to see this dog, you already have so much invested that you'll have a hard time turning him down. Before you make any long-distance plans, then, ask for photos or videos of the dog. Unless you're looking for a specific, hard-to-find bloodline or are planning a coup at Westminster, however, you'll be able to find a very nice dog locally.

Puppy or Adult

One thing to consider when deciding on a Beagle is whether to choose a puppy or an adult. Puppies are wonderful—charming and full of joy. And if your heart is set on one, nothing will stop you. But they are not the right choice for everybody. In the first place, puppies require more attention and vigilance than you think. They also need to be housetrained, and housetraining a Beagle takes longer on the

One of the advantages to choosing an older dog is that his character will already be set.

average than it does for some other breeds. But if you raise your puppy right and he has the correct genetic heritage, he'll grow up secure and confident, and that in itself is worth a lot.

There are advantages to choosing an older dog, too. Beagles are very long-lived dogs, so you don't have to worry that you'll lose him if he's five, eight, or even ten years old. The older dog has a set character, which you will be able to observe right away. In fact, if you obtain your older dog from a reputable shelter or breed rescue, they will already have gauged his temperament and made sure that you and the Beagle are a good match. Be sure that you inquire specifically about the character traits that are of interest to you. The following are some key questions to ask:

- Does the dog chase cats? While Beagles almost never hurt cats, they are chase-oriented and may run after them.
- Is he a barker? Beagles are one of the noisiest of breeds, so you need to know where your prospective pet falls on the bark scale.
- Does he try to escape? All Beagles will run if given their chance; that is their independent hunt nature speaking. But only a few make an active effort to escape their fenced yard.
- How does the dog get along with kids? Women? Men? Most Beagles love everyone, and only a very small minority are aggressive, but some are shy and fearful. This is a genetic defect in some lines and can be ameliorated, although not eliminated, through good training and confidence building.
- What is his activity level? Athlete or couch potato? You can find some of each, although younger Beagles are pretty energetic as a rule.

Beagles are very adaptable, flexible dogs. They are not "one-person" dogs and will quickly learn to love you and your family and get along well in your home. They'll pick up your household routine quite easily. Besides, older dogs usually come already housetrained, and they will almost assuredly sleep calmly through the night. They have gotten over the chewing phase, and some may come already trained to sit, lie down, and fetch your slippers. Because Beagles are the ultimate pack dog, they will quickly figure out who is who in the household and settle quickly into their place. Frequently petting and brushing your Beagle will help him bond to you.

Male or Female

The decision to own a male or female Beagle is really a personal preference. There is no major difference in personality between male and female dogs. Both sexes are friendly, stubborn, charming, and really, really cute.

Breeders

The easiest way to find a good breeder, if you don't have personal contacts, is to check out various Beagle breed clubs near you. The members will be happy to help you locate a good kennel.

Even if you don't know a lot about dogs or dog breeding, you should be able to spot a top-notch facility. A good breeder will have a clean, sheltered facility, preferably indoors. (Beagles raised outdoors may come from a line of hunting Beagles who may not easily adjust to a more sedentary indoor life.) The dogs will be clean, happy, and friendly. They should react positively to you and to the breeder.

Good breeders usually have a line of people waiting to buy puppies, so be prepared to wait. Spend the time reading up on Beagles so you can become an armchair expert. At the very least, study the breed standard and a book or two about dogs in general. The more informed you are, the better choices you will make, and the happier you will be with your dog.

If a breeder doesn't have the type of puppy you are looking for, she should be able to direct you to someone else. Breeders who don't seem to know any other breeders raise red flags. A good breeder can provide references from previous customers. It's a good idea to call these folks and ask questions about the health and temperament of the Beagle they purchased. A breeder who's unwilling to supply references may have something to hide.

The breeder will share with you the goals of her own breeding program. One shortcut I have used to sort out good breeders from bad ones is to ask the simple question, "What are the goals of your breeding program?" If the breeder stares at you blankly, you may want to reconsider buying a dog from her. A responsible breeder, however, once you broach this topic, will not stop talking about it. Ask the breeder how long she has been breeding dogs. Although

A responsible breeder will allow you to meet a puppy's dam and possibly his sire.

every breeder has to begin at some point, inexperienced buyers are best matched with experienced breeders. Ask the breeder how often she breeds; breeders with large numbers of litters over a short period are suspect.

Notice how the breeder interacts with her Beagles. The dogs should seem happy, cheerful, and comfortable around her. If her dogs seem shy, frightened, or reluctant to come close, reconsider buying one of her dogs. Dogs who are not loved are probably not well cared for, either. And although Beagles are remarkably resilient dogs, your life will be made much easier if you choose one who has had a good start in life.

A responsible breeder will allow you to meet a puppy's dam (and possibly sire). This is very important because most dogs inherit their temperament largely from their mothers. Shyness in particular is an inherited trait in Beagles and is quite prevalent in some family lines. A shy mother or father dog suggests that the puppies will also be shy.

It may sound a bit strange, but the best choice of breeder is the so-called hobby breeder. A hobby breeder is no rank amateur but someone who breeds for the love of the breed, not for financial gain. She doesn't depend on selling Beagles for her living. She probably takes her dogs to shows because she is proud of them and of her role in producing them. She enjoys breeding a litter occasionally and is interested in improving her line of Beagles. Selling to the highest bidder isn't on her list of things to do. You won't see dozens and dozens of dogs locked up in a pen in the backyard. A good hobby breeder has made her dogs part of her own family, and her puppies will easily become part of yours.

Show Beagles Versus Field Beagles

Not all Beagle breeders breed for the same reasons: Some breed hunting dogs, some breed show dogs, and some breed field trial dogs. Hunting Beagles are leggier and rangier than the other kinds, even though they're all Beagles. If you just want a jolly family pet and are not interested in hunting or field trials, it's probably smartest to get your dog from a show breeder, one who breeds primarily conformation or field trial rather than hunting dogs. These conformation or field trial type dogs also tend to be calmer. However, if you are planning on hunting, by all means seek out a breeder who specializes in this type of dog, who by the way may not be AKC registered. The world of hunting Beagles is a separate universe.

All Beagles are truly Beagles, however. Show breeders know that their dogs are still, after all these years, hunters first, even though most couldn't really compete in the field. In fact, it's amazing how quickly a show Beagle can forget everything he was taught about showing in the presence of game. I was once at a dog show that was being held on the same grounds (and at the same site) as a 4-H Show. The Beagles and other scenthounds had to pass through an exhibit of rabbits on the way to their ring. The hounds went bonkers, the rabbits nearly had heart attacks, and the show organizers decided to rethink their planning for the following year.

Although there has been an effort to develop a dual-purpose Beagle who can succeed in all areas, most pet owners really only want a companion dog. The truth is that most pet owners would not benefit from having show dogs who more closely resemble hunting Beagles. Most pet owners want a relatively calm dog who doesn't need to be out chasing rabbits every minute. Many hunting Beagles bought as pets eventually end up in shelters because their

If you are looking for a good family pet, it's probably best to get your Beagle from a show breeder.

owners can't handle them. Hunting Beagles may be less "trainable," more destructive in the house, and more stubborn than their show-type brethren. This doesn't mean that hunting Beagles can't make excellent house pets. They can and do. What I mean is that if your heart is set on such a dog, you must be prepared to give him the rigorous exercise and thorough training he needs to keep him happy and busy. Be prepared to work hard and play hard, and you'll all have a super time!

After you have purchased your Beagle, a good breeder will provide you with a signed, written contract, veterinary records, and pedigree. The AKC requires the following information on a signed AKC registration application (called a blue slip), signed bill of sale, or signed written statement:

- Breed, sex, and color of the dog.
- Date of birth of the dog.
- Registered names of the dog's parents.
- Name of the breeder.

Rescues and Shelters

More than 11 million cats and dogs go into shelters every year; more than half never come out. The traditional shelter is a very good place to get a pet, and with an estimated 4 million dogs dumped in them every year, you have plenty of dogs from which to choose. Most Beagles given up to rescues and shelters are between 7 and 12 months of age (the time at which they are most energetic, and their previous owners decided they couldn't handle them).

Finding a responsible shelter or rescue organization is much like finding a good breeder, but in some ways it's easier. While many irresponsible breeders exist, most shelters and rescues are responsible to the maximum. In fact, most shelter and rescue organizations have *higher* standards than breeders do when they select a home for the dogs who come into their care. Shelters and rescue groups will grill you with questions about your lifestyle and ability to care for a needy dog. Not only do they have a long and detailed application form, but most check with your vet and do home visits. They will also call to check on the dog's welfare after adoption, just as human baby adoption agencies do.

A good shelter or rescue organization will be upfront with you about the particular issues each dog may have and will provide support for you during the rehoming process.

Choosing a shelter or rescue dog does not mean you will avoid all puppy-type problems. Some of these dogs are indeed very young, and some may not be fully housetrained. Many Beagles who come into shelters and rescues were raised by hunters. These dogs probably lived outside in a kennel all their lives. Some have never seen the inside of a house, so it's no surprise they aren't housetrained! Also, because shelter or rescue dogs may have already been abandoned or abused once or twice, it's normal for them to be reluctant to offer you their whole devotion right away. Be patient with these dogs, just as you would be patient with a child. They need all of your love and care to make them whole. Beagles who come from shelters may experience shelter shock (the natural depression or uncertainty that accompanies being suddenly thrust from a home environment to a kennel) and a period of intense shyness. Be patient with them—they will blossom!

To help get the best fit between you and your new dog, be honest with the rescue or shelter about what your own lifestyle is like and what traits you are looking for (or would have problems with) in a new pet.

Be sure you take your new Beagle to the veterinarian for a clean bill of health before you introduce him into your home, no matter where the dog came from.

Rescue and shelter dogs require a lot of love and patience as they adjust to their new homes.

If you want to rename your dog, go right ahead. While it may take an older dog a while to figure out what you mean, he'll get it eventually. Dogs don't internalize a name the way we do; they don't identify themselves with that particular combination of phonemes. They simply understand that when you make a certain sound, it means something is happening that concerns them. Thus, you won't hurt his feelings or cause identity confusion, although it is true that unless you really can't stand your Beagle's former name, it's probably easier just to stick with it.

Pet Stores

While it's hard to resist a cute puppy anywhere you find one, use caution before buying a Beagle from a pet store. Pet store dogs may not be as well bred as a dog purchased from a breeder, and consequently, they may have been poorly socialized. This is why it's important to do your research if you decide to purchase your Beagle from a pet store.

One advantage to purchasing your Beagle from a pet store is that oftentimes it is a convenient option. Another advantage to purchasing your Beagle from a pet store is the wide selection available. There are a variety of pet stores from which to choose, but you have to be careful, because some pet stores obtain their stock from unreputable commercial breeders who are more interested in money than in dogs. In most cases, pet store buyers have their pick of many different dogs, and usually the dogs have had at least a minimum of care.

There is a huge variation in quality between pet store dogs who come from the best commercial kennels and ones who come from the worst. As is the case with backyard breeders, you need to do your research and take a good look at the health of the puppies.

Don't be afraid to question the seller of the Beagle the same way you would a breeder. Be sure to request the paperwork you require, including health and pedigree information where applicable.

CHOOSING THE RIGHT BEAGLE FOR YOU

Like people, Beagles are individuals. Each has his own looks and character. Being able to match the individual dog to the perfect owner is sometimes a bit complicated, but you can often facilitate the process through careful observation.

Physical Appearance

Healthy puppies are plump but not potbellied. (A distended belly could signify parasites.) Their ears, skin, and gums should be pink, not red or pale. Puppies should move well even at eight weeks, and they should carry their tails high. They should be clean and smell sweet. The eyes and ears should be free of discharge, and the feces should be well formed, with no sign of diarrhea.

Temperament

You should be able to touch your prospective puppy all over without getting a frightened or hostile response. See how eagerly the puppy will follow you and how responsive he seems to your words and voice. Happy-to-follow-along puppies will be easier to train later on.

Ask someone else to hold the puppy for a moment, and distract his attention. While the puppy is looking away from you, make a sharp noise or drop something. The puppy should react instantly; if he doesn't, further tests on his hearing need to be done. It's important that the puppy be

Healthy Beagle puppies should be clean, smell sweet, and move well.

A Beagle puppy with a good temperament should be friendly, with no sign of shyness.

looking away when you perform this quick test—dogs are extremely good at reading your body language.

Watch the puppy move. While you can't tell too much at this stage, a well-moving puppy is a good sign. Pick up the puppy of your choice and cradle him on his back in your arms, just the way you'd hold a baby. It is best to sit on the floor for complete security. He may struggle a bit and that's okay, but a real fighter may be too independent to be the ideal family pet. As you hold him, see if he makes eye contact with you. A dog who won't make eye contact may grow up to be too timid. The adult Beagle should have many of these same characteristics. Overall, he should be friendly and confident, with no trace of viciousness or shyness.

PAPERWORK

Although buying a puppy is a highly emotional experience, it's also a business deal. You should receive a contract that states what puppy you are buying, his birth date, price, the registered names and numbers of both parents, and the names and contact information for both breeder and buyer.

The contract will also state when you will receive the application for registration (which is as soon as the breeder gets it from the AKC) so that you can register your dog with the AKC. If you have a spay/neuter agreement (often the

Multiple Beagles

Although some breeds of dogs do better when raised singly, Beagles are delightful when raised in twos or even threes. They are the most "packy" of pack dogs and like to be around other Beagles. Some people feel that pairs of puppies tend to bond with each other rather than with their owners, but I have found that this is true more of sporting dogs than with scenthounds. Scenthounds were bred to be pack animals; it's their natural social structure. Just be sure you can afford as many as you choose, and make sure that each puppy receives sufficient attention and training. There is no denying the fact that the only thing cuter than one Beagle is two Beagles—or even three. The great disadvantage of choosing more than one puppy is that two puppies eventually become two elderly dogs. It's often better to have dogs of different ages so that you don't have to deal with the heartbreak of losing both at about the same time.

If you choose to have multiple Beagles, pay attention to your community's rules. The United States Supreme Court wrote over a century ago that communities have the police power to ban dogs outright. Most suburban communities restrict the number of dogs per household to four or five, and some are even stricter. (The community does not have to have "rational basis" for doing so, either. It just can.)

case with a pet-quality, as opposed to a show-quality, pup), that will also be in the contract. If you have a spay/neuter agreement, the breeder may also choose to give you a "limited registration," which means that if you don't hold up your end of the deal and neuter your dog, the puppy won't be eligible for registration. Limited registration can be changed to open registration at any time. This sometimes occurs if the puppy suddenly demonstrates show-dog promise.

Make sure that all guarantees the breeder gives are in writing. These guarantees may refer to present or future medical conditions, such as hip dysplasia. Hips cannot be certified until after the dog is two years old. The acceptable "grade" of the hips should also be included in the contract. Not all reputable breeders will have their Beagles tested for hip dysplasia, however, as this problem is not the scourge in Beagles as it is in some other breeds. However, it can occur.

You should receive a medical record for the puppy that indicates the veterinary care he has received, including deworming, vaccinations, and physical exams. You should also receive a feeding schedule that sets forth the amount and type of food your puppy has been eating. Finally, the breeder should give you a two- to three-day supply of food and a towel or toy the puppy is familiar with.

If possible, you should take your puppy to see your own vet within 48 hours of purchase, especially if the contract

If You Are Allergic

People who suffer allergies to dogs can usually manage to keep them by taking some simple precautions. These include having another (nonallergic) family member take over grooming—outdoors if possible. If there is no one who can do this, consider a professional groomer.

Keep one dog-free area in your home, preferably the bedroom. Studies show that if you can get eight to ten hours of pure breathing during the night, you can handle daytime allergic stress better. Also, get rid of as many rugs and upholstered furniture as possible. This stuff harbors allergens. If you must have upholstered couches and so on, keep your Beagle off of them. Vacuum like mad either with a HEPA vacuum or a regular vacuum with double-layered bags. If you have rugs, though, be careful. Vacuuming can actually stir up the allergens and get them swirling around in the air. Installing hardwood floors or tile with washable rugs is a better plan.

has a clause that allows you to bring the puppy back if your vet determines he is not in good health. The contract should also say how the situation will be remedied.

Don't forget to have the contract signed by all concerned! A good breeder will keep in touch with you about how the puppy is doing and help resolve any problems.

BRINGING YOUR NEW BEAGLE HOME

It's a very exciting thing to add a new dog to your household, but you can't expect your new Beagle to be as thrilled as you are. If you are bringing home a puppy, think of this. His entire life, the one he shared with his mom and brothers and sisters, is gone forever. He has been transported without his consent to a new house with a new family, new sounds, smells, and possibly even other pets! No wonder he's

When you first bring your new Beagle home, provide a low-key but comforting welcome.

a bit uneasy. Older dogs may not understand why they have had to leave their previous home, and dogs from the shelter may be so shelter shocked that they can't feel much of anything for a while. Fear or depression may be a temporary part of your dog's emotional baggage.

As a smart Beagle owner, you will want to

If you have children, show them how to properly interact with the Beagle.

provide a low-key comforting welcome. Plan to bring home your dog on a day when you can spend a lot of time with him. This way, you can begin to bond, and your Beagle can get the feel of your home. Don't push anything. Just let him know where things are, including his crate, which he will soon learn to appreciate as a safe haven. Also, as soon as you get home, walk your Beagle outside and encourage him to eliminate. Praise him mightily, or even offer him a treat for succeeding.

If you have children, you should have already explained the rules for interacting with the new pet, which should include no screaming, stomping around, or pulling his ears or tail. Show them that the new dog should approach them first, and this may take some time. But if you want your dog to become your child's best friend (and he will) let him make the first move.

If you own other pets, you may want to separate them at first using a baby gate. This will allow them to see and smell each other, but it will prevent them from directly interacting with the new Beagle. Beagles are by nature the absolute friendliest and best pack dogs around, so if your other pets are friendly, everyone should get along well almost from the start.

Your first real trouble, especially if you have a puppy, may occur at night, when everyone is ready to go to bed. The dark and quiet may serve to remind your Beagle puppy that

A baby gate is the perfect way to keep your Beagle out of rooms that harbor dangerous items.

his mom and siblings are nowhere in sight or smell range. You can try leaving the radio on, but the puppy will probably cry anyway. Now you must make your decision. You can tough it out and make the dog sleep in his own bed, or you can give in and let the dog sleep in bed with you. The choice is ultimately up to you!

SUPPLIES

Like new babies, new dogs need a plethora of supplies. The following items will help your Beagle settle into his new home.

Baby Gate

Baby or specially designed dog gates are essential for keeping your dog out of any room you don't want him in. If your puppy is a major chewer, though, don't get a wooden baby gate.

Bowls and Dishes

Because your Beagle will need a supply of clean, fresh water at all times, as well as food on a regular basis, he will require his own set of dishes. I prefer to use stainless steel to feed my own dogs—they are inexpensive, tough, and easy to clean. Ceramic dishes are prettier, though, and are also suitable. Both come in weighted varieties that resist being tipped over by a playful puppy, although ceramic ones are breakable. Plastic dishes are not a good choice. First, Beagles can and will chew through cheap plastic, and second, plastic can develop cracks and gaps that harbor dangerous bacteria. Whatever style you choose, you should wash the bowls and

Stainless steel food and water dishes are best because they are tough and easy to clean.

dishes frequently in hot, soapy water, just as you would your own crockery. Beagles deserve no less!

Collar

Your Beagle will need a proper collar, and he should learn how to wear it properly. You can't stick a collar on a young dog and expect him to automatically know all about it. He needs time to figure out what this strange thing is around his neck!

The best kind of collar to put on your Beagle is a simple buckle collar. Choke collars, pinch or prong collars, no-pull harnesses, head halters, and the like are actually training collars for use if simpler methods don't work. (And they will if you are patient and consistent.) In addition, dogs can learn to ignore choke collars, and they will just keep pulling anyway—you will hear them choking. These and pinch or prong collars can be dangerous and painful to your Beagle. Head halters resemble the halters used on horses, and they give you a lot of control as to where his head is. These work, but scenthounds like Beagles just don't like them. They like to smell as they go along, which requires putting the old nose down to the ground. (A dog can walk along easily smelling the ground in a harness or collar, but it's more difficult with a head halter.) No-pull harnesses fit under the dog's front legs with loops over the dog's shoulders. When the dog pulls, the harness pulls the front legs back, thus slowing his pace. If these harnesses are not fitted properly, you can cut off circulation to the legs, however. They can also be hard on the back.

The problem with most harnesses and collars for your dog is that they set up an oppositional reflex—you pull, and the dog pulls back. If you like the idea of a harness for your Beagle, I strongly suggest the simple, highly effective Wayne Hightower harness that has a simple loop in front (not on the back like most collars) to which the leash is attached. This harness allows even the smallest child to control the dog easily without putting any stress on the dog.

Crate

Next to eating, sleeping is the number-one priority on the agenda of most dogs, and a crate is a safe, comfortable place for that activity. Although crates may look like cages, a properly brought up Beagle has no such prejudice. He thinks of the crate as a safe haven and a den of his own. In addition, a crate is a great housetraining tool, not a place of banishment. Dogs should not be locked in their crates for more than two hours except at night when they should be sleeping. This doesn't mean your dog *has* to sleep in a crate, of course. Mine never do. But he should be taught to accept a comfortable crate when asked. This is important for traveling or when the dog is sick and needs to have his activity restricted, or when you want to keep him away from Cousin Ethel's bratty kids.

Crates come in three basic styles: wire mesh, sturdy fiberglass or plastic, and fold-up nylon mesh. Each has its

A crate, such as the Nylabone® Fold-Away Den & Carrier™, can be used for housetraining and to provide a safe haven for your Beagle puppy.

distinct advantages, and many dog owners eventually end up with one of each. Your Beagle's crate should be not only high enough for him to stand up in but big enough for him to turn around in easily and stretch out in completely.

The wire crate offers the best ventilation and vision. Once inside, your dog can look around and see what's happening. This type of crate is wonderful in the summer, because it allows fresh air to circulate. On the other hand, it offers no protection from the sun (unless you drape it with a towel) or cold wind. The fiberglass or plastic crate, like the Nylabone Fold-Away Den & Carrier, is very tough and good for traveling and sleeping. It provides the most den-like atmosphere, and many dogs feel especially secure in one. The new fold-up nylon mesh crates are indispensable for traveling and quick setup. They can go anywhere! Their main disadvantage is that a dog not used to crates can tear them with his claws.

Whatever crate you choose, be forewarned: The crate is not a Beagle sitter! Beagles are hunting dogs, and most today are terribly underexercised. To keep them out of trouble, many people stick them into crates, where they receive even less exercise, become more unruly when released, and are

If You Lose Your Beagle

Because they are wanderers, Beagles are even less likely to return home than are other dogs if they escape. And even when they are noticed wandering around a neighborhood, people often don't call authorities the way they might if they saw a wandering Rottweiler or Pit Bull. They just don't feel threatened enough to worry about it. On the other hand, a Beagle is such a friendly dog that if you're lucky, someone might find him and immediately call you.

To help make your life easier in the event that your Beagle should become lost, keep a recent color photo of your dog on file, one that shows his markings. It actually doesn't hurt to preprint "Lost Dog" posters, just in case. Leave a space at the bottom to write when he was last seen. The bigger the print, the better. However, don't crowd the flyer with so much information that it's difficult to read. It may also be a good idea to write that your dog needs medication, just in case he is picked up by someone who considers keeping him. This may give them pause—do they want a sick dog? It doesn't matter that your Beagle is not really sick. You just want him back! If your Beagle does become lost, start looking for him immediately. The longer he's gone, the less likely he will be found. Usually, a dog will travel no more than 1 mile from home in any direction on the first day. But the second it may be 2 miles, and so on. Contact your shelter and all the local vet offices in case he has been brought there. I would actually go to the shelter. Many shelter workers may not know a Beagle from a Borzoi. Place posters everywhere, including vet clinics. Enlist the help of neighborhood kids and offer a reward. Give them instructions, too. If your dog is shy, tell them just to keep an eye on him while they send someone to get you. Otherwise, they may try to chase the dog, and he could run away from them.

then thrust back into their crates, and the vicious cycle continues.

After you have chosen the right crate for you and your dog, be sure to provide a soft, cushy, washable mat for his sleeping comfort. When you are housetraining, however, you may want to omit the mat. Dogs are often driven to urinate on soft, absorbable surfaces, for obvious reasons.

Exercise Pen

This portable puppy playpen is a compromise between the isolation of the crate and the free range of the kitchen or living room. During times when you want your puppy around you but not out of sight, the so-called x-pen ("x" is for "exercise") is a great way to oversee your puppy. While you are cooking dinner or cleaning the refrigerator, your puppy can watch you. Even more important, you can keep an eye on him.

Identification

Every year, 8 to 10 million pets are lost or stolen, according to the AKC's Animal Recovery Program. Only a small fraction ever return home. To help prevent this from happening to your Beagle, get him some visible identification in the way of a collar and dog tag with your current home and cell phone numbers. This is your first line of defense, no matter what other kind of ID you use.

A tattoo is another option, and it's a permanent identifier. This may be good or bad, for obvious reasons. If your dog is found by a knowledgeable person or turned over to a shelter, they will look for the tattoo, which is generally located on the inside of the left leg or on the abdomen. The tattoo is usually a special registry number, but I know people who have used their phone numbers. Not all vets do tattooing, however. Another downside of the tattoo is that lost Beagles may be too scared to allow a stranger to examine them when trying to look for the tattoo.

A third option is a microchip implant, in which an ID chip the size of a grain of rice is implanted between your dog's shoulder blades. Each chip is encrypted with a unique and unalterable identification code. It will last for the life of your dog. If your dog is found, the chip can be read by a scanner wand possessed by most vet and shelters. The problem with this method of ID is that someone has to know it's there and have the equipment to read it. In addition, more than one company makes these chips, and as of this date, they are not interchangeable. So the vet or shelter needs to try all three "wands" to find out whose dog he is.

Noseprint identification represents the newest technology. Just as human beings have unique fingerprints, dogs have unique noseprints. With noseprint identification, the dog's nose impression is scanned, placed on an ID card with the dog's picture and information, and stored on a nationwide database.

Leash

You'll need a regular 6-foot lead for your Beagle, but you may also want to get a longer one for when you have more room. Choose leather or study nylon, never clanking, noisy chains. Some people even like flexible-type leads.

A leather or sturdy nylon leash is the best choice for your Beagle.

Teach your puppy to accept the lead by leaving a short one on him for a while. Supervise him the entire time so that he doesn't catch the lead on anything or chew it to pieces. He will probably fuss with it a bit at first, but he'll soon get used to it. When you do pick up the end, follow *him* for a while. When you take the lead yourself, call the puppy to you gently; when he toddles up to you, give him a treat and praise him. Very soon he will be happily following you everywhere. At this stage, try not to struggle with your puppy. If he resists, don't tug the other way, but don't give in either. Lure him to you with a biscuit. He'll soon catch on that it's fun to do what he's asked. Keep puppy lessons short—five minutes a couple of times a day is enough.

Toys

Dogs, especially puppies, need to gnaw. It helps them explore their world and relieves teething discomfort. That's where toys come in, unless of course, you want your dog eating your underwear and gobbling your designer handbag.

Choose toys that do not have small, easily removable parts, and throw them away as soon as they start to fall apart. Toys (especially balls) that are too small can be

Choose toys for your Beagle that are durable and too large to be accidentally swallowed.

swallowed easily. Nylabones, latex squeaky toys, rubber bones and balls, and faux lamb's wool plush toys are all excellent choices. However, not all puppies are equal, and not all should have the same toys. Destructive chewers should be given only durable hard rubber or nylon toys. Aggressive but not destructive chewers are safe with canvas, fleece, or plush toys. Don't buy too many in the beginning, though, as your dog may become overwhelmed or bored— rotate them and keep enough around to prevent your pup from chewing on the forbidden furniture.

You may want to avoid stick-type rawhide chews, as they can become stuck in your dog's throat. In addition, refrain from giving your Beagle toys that require batteries, because he could swallow them.

PUPPY-PROOFING YOUR HOME

All puppies are curious, and all puppies get into trouble. In fact, the trouble they can get into is limited only by their imagination and reach. Because we humans are the ones with the opposable thumbs, it's up to us to dog-proof the house, the same as we would for a new baby or toddler.

Puppies learn about their environment by mouthing things and chewing on objects. This is normal behavior that continues until adulthood and even beyond. This is why it's so important to keep your Beagle safe by puppy-proofing as much as you can both inside and outside your home.

Indoors

Your house is a veritable garden of temptation for a curious puppy: smelly sneakers, interesting electrical cords, window cords and drapes, medicines, you name it. A good way to puppy-proof your home is to look at it from a Beagle's eye view. You may have to crawl around a bit yourself. Lock away valuable keepsakes and dangerous cleaners. Keep doors shut to areas you want to remain off-limits, especially closets and cabinets. Hide electric cords, or tape them to the wall and spray them with an anti-chew spray. Keep kitchen supplies like aluminum and plastic food wrap away from your puppy, as they can be very dangerous to your dog. (These items are very tempting to Beagles because they smell like food, and Beagles are very food oriented.) If ingested, aluminum foil can cut a dog's intestines, causing internal bleeding. Plastic food wrap can cause choking or intestinal obstruction. In addition, all trash cans should be made inaccessible. Highly scented items (flowers, trash, candles) are irresistible. Older dogs are not apt to chew them, but young ones will. Finally, potentially toxic foods, like chocolate, should be kept away from your dog. Chocolate contains a toxic substance called theobromine that can poison your dog, causing symptoms like vomiting, diarrhea, tremors, hyperactivity, and seizures. Dark and unsweetened baking chocolates are especially dangerous. Tobacco is another common poison that can be lethal to pets. For most poisonings, there isn't much you can do at home. Call your veterinarian or veterinary emergency facility if you suspect your pet has been poisoned.

Outdoors

Beagles really enjoy being outside, more so than many other dogs. That doesn't mean, however, that you should lock him out in the yard night and day. Beagles are family dogs and like to be with you. It's all very well to keep a hunting dog in a kennel, for these animals get plenty of exercise and company day after day while you're on the game trail. However, if you're not out there hunting with your Beagle three or four times a week, he needs to live in the house with you. Even if you do hunt, your dog still prefers to cuddle up with you at night. Indulge him in this. It's the least you can do.

Scoop That Poop!
It's important to pick up after your pet not only when walking, but also after your Beagle has eliminated in the yard. Picking up the feces helps keep the soil free of roundworms, whipworms, and hookworms, which is healthier for everyone.

A sturdy, secure fence is the best way to keep your Beagle safe in the yard.

Fencing

A safe Beagle yard is a fenced-in yard. Unsecured Beagles turn into wandering Beagles, who turn into lost Beagles. The fence must be strong and secure, as Beagles are good at digging or climbing their way out. It may seem excessive, but Beagles are such good climbers and diggers that a 6-foot fence is really your best bet. If your Beagle is a digger, add some chicken wire underground to a depth of at least 2 feet. The top portion of the wire will be attached to the fence.

A tie-out or chain is not an acceptable substitute for a fence. Dogs kept on a chain feel vulnerable and scared. They don't get exercise, and they are prime candidates for dognappers and abusive children. Dogs can entangle themselves in a chain and do themselves serious injury as well. A brief, supervised period on a stake is acceptable, but your dog should not be left unattended. Beagles resent being tied and can become destructive or self destructive if left tied outside.

An "invisible fence" is not a safe alternative, because it doesn't keep out strange, bullying dogs or kids. You can keep a Beagle without a fenced yard if you are committed to getting out and walking him on a leash several times a day. However, you just can't let him loose outside if you don't have a fence.

Chemicals

Never allow your pup in the garage without close supervision. Ethylene-glycol antifreeze, fertilizers, pesticides, paint, and nails are lurking there just waiting to kill your dog. If ingested, sweet-tasting antifreeze is often fatal, even in tiny amounts. Poisoning from antifreeze is a serious medical emergency that must be treated by a veterinarian immediately.

If you use an insecticide or other chemicals on your lawn, follow label instructions to the letter. Allow the product to dry before permitting pets and people into the yard. Most products are safe once they are dry and bound to the grass.

Ice-melting chemicals and salt placed across sidewalks and roads can cause severe burning to your dog's footpads. Whenever possible, avoid walking your dog through these substances, and wash off his footpads when you return home from your winter walks. There are also products available that can be applied to your dog's footpads prior to going outside that may help reduce the pain that is often caused by road salt and chemicals.

Flowers and Plants

Many common flowers, bulbs, and bushes (like boxwood) are poisonous to dogs. This is why you should never let the puppy explore on his own until you have inspected the yard first. Choose an area of the yard that will serve as your puppy's potty area. This is more convenient for both of you. It makes it easier for him to identify the acceptable elimination area and also lessens the possibility of you stepping in something untoward.

Only after you have inspected the yard for poisonous flowers and plants should you allow your Beagle into the backyard.

Insects

Don't forget the fleas, ticks, and mosquitoes that may be living in your yard. Get rid of flea hotels, like piles of grass clippings. Fleas like dark, warm, moist places rich in organic debris. Ticks like taller grass and brush, so keep the lawn clipped. You may also want to spray with pesticides developed especially for ticks. Mosquitoes are fans of standing, stagnant water, so get rid of anything that holds water, including birdbaths and wading pools, unless you change the water at least every 72 hours. If you have a pond, stock some goldfish in it; they'll eat mosquito eggs and larvae.

Cold Weather

Although dogs are covered with fur and can handle some cold easily, remember that size counts. Small dogs with fairly short hair, like Beagles, are not as good at handling the cold as Malamutes. Other risk factors include age (older dogs and puppies most at risk), sick or underweight dogs, dogs with poor circulation or diabetes, prolonged exposure, wet dogs, a cramped position, or previous cold-related injuries, like frostbite.

If your dog does spend a lot of time running around outside, be sure to give him extra calories to stoke his internal energies. Otherwise, he may need less food, as most dogs are less active in the winter.

After your Beagle has been outside for a romp or walk, clean any lime rock or calcium chloride salt that may be lodged between his toes. If he starts licking it off, he could be in for a bout of vomiting and diarrhea.

Hot Weather

Beagles can handle warm weather better than some other breeds, but they are not tropical animals. They need access to fresh, cool water and shade during the hot months.

TRAVELING WITH YOUR BEAGLE

Life is so much more fun if you can take your Beagle wherever you go. Of course, you will have to obey the rules of common courtesy first. If you're going to stay with friends, ask in advance if your Beagle is welcome. The same goes for hotels, motels, and campgrounds. Don't just show up without first making sure pets are allowed and finding out what the rules regarding them are.

If you are lucky enough to secure a pet-friendly hotel, be considerate of the other guests. Don't allow your dog to mark the furniture, bark his head off, or defecate without you cleaning it up. If you have to leave your Beagle alone in a hotel room, put a "Do Not Disturb" sign on the door and tell the front desk there is a dog inside. Most hotels require that the animal be crated while in the room, especially if you won't be there.

Always make sure your Beagle is properly vaccinated for the area in which you are traveling. For example, leptospirosis is common in some areas but nonexistent in others. Check with your vet to make sure your dog is up-to-date on any shots he may need. Take his vet records and recent photos in case he gets lost.

Also, double-check all identification tags. The tags should include a way to reach you or someone who knows where you are. It doesn't do any good to have the person who located your dog call your home if you aren't going to be there.

When traveling with your Beagle, make sure he is properly vaccinated for the area in which you are traveling.

It's also a good idea to take a simple first-aid kit with you, including a safe antidiarrhea medication. Dogs tend to get diarrhea on trips either from the excitement or the strange water. You should also bring along important phone numbers, including that of your veterinarian, the number of the national pet poison control hotline (US: 1-888-4ANI-HELP), and a 24-hour emergency veterinary hospital near where you'll be staying.

Traveling by Car

Most Beagles enjoy travel by car, but if your dog is not accustomed to it, take him for some practice runs before the big day. Feed him about one third of what you normally would before starting out to reduce the chances of him getting sick. However, bring some extra food or snacks with you.

Put your Beagle in a crate or safety harness in the backseat. You don't want him to turn into a football flying through the windshield when you brake for a deer. If traveling by car in the summer months, keep your dog cool by putting icepacks in his crate. Make sure the crate is well ventilated.

Whenever you take your Beagle out, think, "Hmm…what if my car breaks down on the road?" Be prepared for that happenstance. Your travel plans should always include bringing along a leash, a supply of drinking water, and a bowl. If you're traveling during the warmer months, bring a cooling vest or towel that can be wetted, a kiddie pool that can be unfolded, 5 gallons of water (for the kiddie pool), and shade netting or a sun shade.

Even if you don't break down, be prepared to stop about once every two hours. And of course, you should never leave your Beagle in a hot car, not even for a few minutes. Temperatures can soar to 120°F in a closed car even with the windows partway open. Temperatures below freezing are also dangerous for your Beagle. In addition, under no circumstances should you permit your Beagle to ride with his head hanging outside the car windows, charming as the sight might be to fellow drivers. First, you might cause an accident. Even worse, debris or other particles can get into your dog's eyes, injuring or infecting them.

Carsickness

While most Beagles love to travel, some don't and experience carsickness. In a few instances, carsickness has a physical basis, usually a problem in the inner ear, which can often be safely remedied with an over-the-counter product. Ginger can also be effective. More often, though, the cause of carsickness is psychological. Perhaps the dog associates riding in the car with unpleasantness (like going to the vet). Or, perhaps he is frightened of the noise or motion of the car. Sometimes it's hard to figure exactly what came first, the sickness or the fear. Dogs who are anxious may express their anxiety through sickness, and those who get sick in the car may become increasingly anxious about it. Usually (not always), if the dog shows signs of anxiety (slavering, shaking) before even getting into the car, the problem is most likely anxiety based.

To help your dog overcome fear of the car, take it slow and make the car a happy place. Try feeding him treats inside the car while the car is not running. Do this often enough for the dog to regard the car with approval. If your dog is afraid to even approach the car, you'll just have to give treats closer and closer to the car until he finally overcomes his fear. This may take some time.

After you've done this, repeat the routine with the car running. Go slow, as trying to hurry the desensitization will backfire on you. When you actually start moving, go for *very* short trips to somewhere nice, even if it's only a block. Get out and walk the dog. Do this every day until the dog starts to really look forward to his daily car rides.

If your dog still retains his fear of the car, you may have to resort to a medical solution. Nonprescription products may help. In a few cases, you may need to get out the big guns and ask the vet for an antianxiety medication.

Traveling by Air

Everyone has horror stories about lost or injured pets on a flight, but you can reduce the risk of potential harm by following the law and using common sense. You will generally be required to supply a health certificate (not more than ten days old), which can be obtained from your veterinarian, and a valid rabies certificate before you'll be allowed to fly.

When traveling by air, try to book a nonstop, midweek flight. Try to fly during the evening or morning when it will be coolest.

Most airlines are also quite picky about the crate your Beagle will be flying in. General rules are that the crate must:

- be big enough to allow the dog to stand (without touching the top of the cage), turn around, and lie down;
- have handles;
- have a leak-proof flooring covered with absorbent material;
- be clearly labeled with your name, home address, home telephone number, and destination contact information, as well as a designation of "Live Animal" with letters at least 1 inch high and arrows indicating the crate's upright position;
- be ventilated on opposite sides, with exterior rims and knobs so that airflow is not impeded.

Get the crate well in advance so that your dog can get used to it before the big trip. And make sure your dog is flown as "baggage" (bad as that sounds) rather than as "freight" (which is worse). If he goes as freight, he may be shipped on a different plane. Finally, keep your dog's nails short for the trip; you don't want them getting snagged in the carrier door.

Airline flight regulations with regard to pets change all the time. Contact the air carrier in advance for specific instructions.

Traveling by Bus or Train

Unfortunately, in most states it's illegal for dogs other than service dogs to ride public transport. But check around, you never know.

IF YOU CAN'T TAKE YOUR BEAGLE

It is not always possible or even desirable to take your Beagle along on every trip you take. In that case, you'll need to have a plan. If you're lucky, you can pop him over to a relative's house, but that's not an option for everyone.

Vet Boarding

One option is to board your pet. Some veterinary clinics also run boarding facilities, which is your best choice if your dog has a medical condition that requires regular medication, or if the dog may have seizures. However, most

Pet Travel Scheme (PETS)

PETS is a system that permits companion animals from certain countries to travel to the UK without undergoing a period of quarantine. This scheme also applies to people in the UK who want to travel with their pets to other European Union countries. For more information, visit the Department for Environment Food and Rural Affairs' website at www.defra.gov.uk.

If you are unable to take your Beagle with you on vacation, consider using a commercial kennel.

boarding facilities at vet clinics are rather spartan and don't offer the opportunities for play and interaction that the best boarding kennels do.

Boarding Kennel

If you decide to use a commercial kennel, ask for a tour before you commit yourself—but commit early. Most kennels fill up a month in advance. Check when you will be able to pick up your dog. Many do not have Sunday pickup. Good kennels:

- are clean and free of excrement;
- have both indoor and outdoor runs (preferably with solid partitions between them);
- allow dogs frequent access to exercise and play;

- provide appropriate grooming and bathing services;
- require proof of vaccination, including bordetella;
- have a vet clinic nearby for emergencies;
- allow you to bring your dog's own food, bedding, and toys if you desire;
- are heated and air-conditioned.

In the United States, a good kennel should be accredited with the American Boarding Kennels Association.

Pet Sitter

Another option is a dog-sitting service. Some services will house-sit as well as pet-sit; others will make arrangements to come in and walk, feed, and play with your dog. If you are thinking of hiring a pet sitter, make sure to meet her first and note how she interacts with your Beagle. Ask for references, experience, and check her ability to walk, or if necessary, medicate your dog. You may also want to test her knowledge by asking how she might handle certain dog problems, like vomiting or diarrhea. If you like the candidate, make specific arrangements as to when she will be coming to care for your dog and what else she might be able to do (like get the mail). Be sure that your pet sitter gets your contact information and that of your veterinarian.

You really can't say you've lived until you've added a Beagle to your family. If all this preparation seems like a lot of work, it's not. It's all part of the fun of life with a Beagle!

FEEDING
YOUR BEAGLE

Nutrition is a cornerstone of good health. It affects the way your dog looks, feels, and behaves. When dogs were wolves, they managed to find proper (although sometimes inadequate) nutrition on their own. Nowadays, they depend totally upon you. Your nutritional choices for your dog determine to a large extent how healthy and happy he will be. This is not a responsibility to take lightly.

NUTRIENTS

A nutrient is a dietary component that has a particular function. Nutrients the body can manufacture on its own from other nutrients are called "nonessential." Those the body needs to import in their final form are called "essential."

Nutrients perform one or more of the following functions:
- Provide energy.
- Act as structural components.
- Take part in the chemical activities of the body.
- Transport substances around the body.
- Maintain body temperature.

There are six basic classes of nutrients: water, proteins, fats, carbohydrates, vitamins, and minerals. Of these, proteins, fats, and carbohydrates provide energy. Water, minerals, and vitamins, although necessary for survival, do not supply energy. The nutrients your dog needs work synergistically. For example, a specific metabolic reaction may take ten steps, each requiring a different nutrient. If even *one* of these nutrients is missing or deficient, it's as if all ten are missing.

Water

Water is the most important substance of all, having the following functions:
- Carries nutrients.
- Flushes waste.
- Aids certain chemical reactions.
- Helps regulate body temperature.

- Provides shape and resilience to the body.

About 70 percent of your dog's lean body mass is water. The percentage of water present in your dog's body depends somewhat on how fat he is. Lean dogs have a higher percentage of water than overweight dogs do, because fat contains less water than muscle tissue. Lean dogs also need proportionately more water because they eat more food per unit of body weight.

Your dog maintains his water balance through water intake and metabolic water production (making water from his food). Water is lost through panting and elimination. Some factors that can influence your dog's need for water include ambient temperature, food type and amount, exercise, certain illnesses, and lactation.

Unless advised by your vet, don't restrict your dog's access to water, even if you think he doesn't really need as much as he is drinking. (One exception may be when housetraining your pup; you may limit his water access for an hour or so before bedtime.) Your Beagle needs constant access to clean, fresh water. If you have more than one Beagle, each dog should have a separate dish.

Proteins

Proteins are long, complex molecules of amino acids, strung together like beads on a chain. They compose about 50 percent of every cell. Proteins are critical in building

Because water is lost through panting and elimination, it is important to ensure that your Beagle has access to plenty of fresh, clean water at all times.

enzymes, hormones, hemoglobin, and antibodies. All animals need protein for maintenance, and young animals need it for growth. If a puppy doesn't get enough protein, his tissues and organs won't develop properly. Dogs also use protein for energy. Dogs with cancer, trauma, and burns need additional protein to help heal.

Fats

Fats have twice the number of calories per gram as proteins or carbohydrates, and they are packed with energy. They keep cells in good working order and add both palatability and texture to food. Dogs digest fats *very* efficiently; about 90 to 95 percent are digested. This percentage is higher than for carbohydrates or protein.

Dogs can use both plant and animal fats with equal ease. However, oils derived from plants provide large amounts of essential fatty acids (EFAs). These acids are essential for many biological functions.

Performance dogs need more fat in their diets than the sedentary Beagle. These dogs also need a highly digestible

A performance diet should have meat with a highly digestible, quality protein source as its first ingredient. To help a dog get off to a good start nutritionally, owners should ideally begin feeding a performance diet 8 to 12 weeks before training begins.

A performance Beagle will need more fat in his diet than a sedentary Beagle.

meat protein as the first ingredient in their food. If you are going to do performance work, however, remember that you have to give the body enough time to respond. Don't think you can feed your Beagle an inexpensive food until the day of the show or hunt. You need to start at least two months before the event.

Carbohydrates

Sugars and starches are both carbohydrates. These carbohydrates, contained in a crystalline granule formation, are found primarily in plants. In fact, in its raw state, between 60 and 90 percent of a plant is composed of carbohydrates (excluding water).

There is no minimum dietary level for carbohydrates in the canine diet. However, when present, they perform the following functions (which can also be performed by proteins and fats):

- Provide energy.
- Supply a heat source for the body when they are metabolized for energy to carbon dioxide and water.
- Serve as building blocks for other biological components, such as glycoproteins, vitamin C, nonessential amino acids, glycolipids, and lactose.
- Can be stored as glycogen or converted to fat.
- Help regulate protein and fat metabolism.

Minerals

Dietary minerals are classed into three groups: macrominerals (sulfur, calcium, phosphorus, magnesium, and the electrolytes sodium, potassium, and chloride), which are consumed in gram amounts per day; trace minerals (iron, zinc, copper, iodine, and selenium), which are needed in milligram or microgram amounts per day (these "microminerals" can be toxic if taken in high doses); and ultratrace minerals (like beryllium), which have been shown to be necessary in laboratory animals but not in dogs.

Minerals participate in nearly every function of the body. They build teeth and bone, serve as enzyme cofactors, and are a vital part of the blood and other body fluids. Minerals also play a role in muscle contraction, the transmission of nerve impulses, and in cell membrane permeability. One of the unusual things about minerals is the way in which they interact. The action of one often enhances, is necessary for, or impedes the action of another. These interactions can occur during digestion, at the tissue storage site, during transport out of the digestive system, or even within the pathways of excretion.

Not every mineral in the world has importance in the diet. Some, like cadmium, lead, and mercury, are harmful in any amounts, and gold and silver, while not harmful, don't do your dog any good, either. (This is a good thing, because gold supplements would cost a lot more than calcium supplements!)

It is very tricky to supplement minerals, because supplementation of any one mineral can create imbalances or interfere with another. While supplementation is sometimes needed to correct an imbalance, this is something that should be addressed in consultation with your veterinarian.

Consult with your veterinarian before supplementing your Beagle's diet with minerals.

Vitamins

Vitamins are plant- and animal-derived substances necessary for your dog's health. Your dog needs only an infinitesimal amount of vitamins in his diet, but that tiny amount is absolutely essential. To qualify as a bona fide vitamin, a substance must be:

- An organic compound different from proteins, fats, or carbohydrates.
- A component of the diet.
- Critical for normal body functioning and whose absence produces a deficiency syndrome.
- Not synthesized in quantities sufficient to support normal physiologic function.

Vitamins are divided into two types: fat soluble (A, D, E, and K) and water soluble (C and the eight B vitamins). Fat-soluble vitamins need dietary fat in order to be absorbed from the gut and taken up into the body, while water-soluble vitamins need only water. Fat-soluble vitamins are handled by the body in the same way as dietary fat—the metabolites of these vitamins are excreted in the feces. Excess fat-soluble vitamins are stored in the liver and can be toxic if too much is eaten. Water-soluble vitamins (except for B_{12}) are not stored in the body and need to be replaced regularly. Most water-soluble vitamins are absorbed in the small intestine and excreted in the urine.

Vitamins play one or more of these roles in the body:

- Act as potentiators or cofactors in enzymatic reactions.
- Help synthesize DNA.
- Scavenge free radicals.
- Release energy from nutrients.
- Maintain cell membrane integrity.
- Help bone development.
- Help maintain calcium homeostasis.
- Aid normal eye function.
- Help nerve impulse transduction.
- Help blood clot.

FEEDING METHODS

You have three basic choices when it comes to serving grub: free feeding, timed feeding, and food-restricted meal feeding. For the Beagle, food-restricted meal feeding is the best.

The amount you feed your dog should depend on his activity level and particular metabolism. I suggest that you follow the manufacturer's feeding labels; 1 cup of one food is not the same calorie-wise as that of another. Observe how your dog does when following the manufacturer's recommendations, and add or decrease the amount of food as needed.

Free Feeding

When free feeding, you simply put down all the food your dog could reasonably be expected to eat during the day and forget about it. Obviously, this is the easiest method for you, but it's not usually a good idea, especially if you have multiple dogs. The dominant dog may get all the food and leave the more submissive dogs without anything to eat. In addition, a free-fed dog in a multiple-dog household who goes off his feed may not be noticed for several days.

Free feeding also encourages a dog to eat throughout the day. Not only is this unnatural, it also causes your dog to be more lethargic and get less exercise because he's burning up calories digesting his food. Consequently, you can end up with an overweight dog.

Timed Feeding

With timed feeding, you give your dog a certain period of time to eat, usually between 10 and 15 minutes, then take the

The best feeding schedule for your Beagle is a food-restricted meal plan; this plan allows you to control your dog's food intake while allowing him to eat at his own pace.

food away. Most dogs eat their entire dinner in a minute or so anyway, so this method is primarily used by people who are dealing with a picky eater. Timed feeding may encourage a picky eater to eat better, but the disadvantage is that you have to stand around timing your dog.

Food-Restricted Meal Feeding

The best choice for most owners is the food-restricted meal feeding. Simply serve the dog his dinner and walk away. Pick up the empty bowl later. This method gives you control over the dog's intake and doesn't put an unnatural pressure on him to "eat up" or else not have anything to eat at all.

Most experts believe feeding two smaller meals a day is better than one large one. There is some evidence that dogs fed only one large meal a day produce more stomach acid; this can lead to irritation of the esophagus. On the other hand, wild dogs are lucky to eat even once a day. But who knows what their esophagi look like?

DOG FOOD LABELS

Dog food labels are regulated by not one but several branches of the US government, including the Food and Drug Administration (FDA) and the Department of Agriculture. In some ways, the labels are more strictly regulated than what goes *inside* the can or bag.

Pet food labels have two main parts: the information panel and the principal display panel.

Information Panel

The information panel contains a list of ingredients, the guaranteed analysis, feeding instructions, and nutritional adequacy claim. Look for a statement on the bag that says that the product successfully passed feeding trials of the Association of American Feed Control Officials (AAFCO). This ensures that the food has at least the minimum amount of nutritional value your dog needs. These trials require that specific data, including information on weight maintenance and bloodwork, be collected from dogs put on the diet for an extended period: ten months for growth formulas and six months for adult formulas. This is supposed to ensure that the food has no nutritional deficiencies or excesses that could be detrimental to your pet in the long run. Of course, six or even ten months isn't that long, but it's better than nothing.

The ingredient list specifies the ingredients in descending order by weight. The guaranteed analysis lists the minimum amounts of certain nutrients like protein. It also lists the percentage of crude fat, crude fiber, and moisture in the ingredients. This can be misleading. It doesn't say where the protein comes from, which is not good, because animal protein is a lot higher quality than plant protein. In addition, some animal proteins (such as that found in hair) are not digestible. The feeding instructions list how much to feed per day. I wouldn't pay much attention to these, however. Dogs are very individual, and the package generally tells you to overfeed, at least in my experience. The nutritional adequacy claim specifies that the food provides compete and balanced nutrition for a particular life stage.

Principal Display Panel

The principal display panel contains the brand name, the name of the meats used, and the age group for which the food is intended. It will say what species the food is for, and the weight of the product will also be included. The product name is subject to AAFCO regulations on the statement of food ingredients.

There are all kinds of arcane rules about how companies can name their foods. For example, if the label states that it is, for instance, "Lamb Dog Food" (*food* is the operant word), it must be 95 percent lamb, exclusive of the water sufficient for processing. No dry food meets this standard, but if it uses a word like "dinner" or "entree" rather than "food," it needs to be only 25 percent lamb. If it uses the words "with lamb," it need only contain 3 percent lamb. If the word "flavor" is used, it means that merely the flavor of the food must be detectable to dogs. Nowhere on the label will you find the actual percentages.

TYPES OF FOOD

Dogs are designed behaviorally to enjoy a wide variety of foods, just as humans are. This sensible practice has helped them survive through hard times over the millennia. And like humans, although they can thrive on one balanced food year in and year out, they would prefer a change. Beagles in particular enjoy more kinds of food than most. This is a food-adventurous breed, to say the least.

Feeding your dog a variety of foods increases the chance that he is getting complete nutrition. Variety also gives the dog's digestive system a workout and makes his eating

Feeding your dog a variety of foods will increase the chance that he is getting complete nutrition.

experience more pleasant, natural, and interesting. Like healthy people, healthy dogs thrive on variety, although a few exhibit signs like vomiting, diarrhea, belching, or flatulence. (This might mean that your dog's digestive system isn't all that it should be.) If you wish to be more cautious, you can change your Beagle's food over a three- to seven-day period. You may take even longer if the diet change is really significant or if your dog has reacted poorly to food changes in the past. Change your dog's diet by gradually mixing in the new food with the old until the change is complete.

A highly variable diet is so palatable to dogs that you may notice your dog gaining weight, simply because he is for the first time really enjoying his food. If that's the case, cut back on the amount he is eating while making sure he is getting a full array of nutrients.

Commercial Foods

Dog food should taste good, at least to the dogs. If you have to lure, beg, bribe, or threaten an otherwise healthy dog to eat commercial food, it probably isn't very tasty, and

Varying the Diet

Don't get trapped into feeding your dog only one food, even a good one. Here's why:

- **It's unnatural.** Dogs are hunters and scavengers by nature and are designed to feed upon a wide variety of foodstuffs.
- **It's boring.** Dogs don't like the same food day in and day out any more than we would.
- **It may be unhealthy.** Studies have not been done long enough on a large enough number of dogs to guarantee that any single food is completely adequate by itself.
- **It may cause allergies.** Researchers believe that one of the best ways for your dog to avoid a food allergy is to consume a wide variety of foods from puppyhood on.
- **It may be impossible.** Your dog may become allergic to something in the food, the company may go out of business, or they may change the formula.

you're creating unneeded stress for both of you. You probably won't experience this problem with your Beagle, though. Beagles are such indiscriminate eaters that they won't give you any hint that the food you're feeding them is really terrible. This is why he depends on you to choose the healthiest food, because he'll eat anything. If you do have the rare picky Beagle, some will say, "Well, just keep offering him the food long enough, and don't give him anything else—he'll eat it eventually." Your dog probably would, rather than starve to death, but that doesn't mean he'll find mealtime enjoyable. Others claim that offering a less palatable food will lead your pet to consume less food. This seems ridiculous to me. Eating is one of life's great joys. Keep your dog trim by feeding him just the right amount of nutritious, tasty food that he requires. If he's getting fat, feed him less and exercise him more. The only reason I can think of for

Keep your dog at a healthy weight by feeding him nutritious food in the proper balance.

serving less palatable foods would be to slow down a greedy dog's eating rate.

Most pet food manufacturers perform palatability studies comparing the target brand of food with other kinds. However, be aware that some dog foods are made *artificially* palatable by the inclusion of ingredients that not only provide no benefit but may actually be harmful to your pet. Artificial flavor enhancers include sugars, digests, processed meat flavors, yeast products, garlic, cheese, and bacon flavors, as well as "masking" flavors designed to hide the odor of the original food.

Rather than give a list of poor-quality dog foods, here are some ingredients you may want to avoid in a variety of foods:

- **Artificial preservatives.** Artificial preservatives include things like propyl gallate, BHA, BHT, and ethoxyquin. Not only do some dogs react adversely to these preservatives, but there are serious questions about their safety. Choose foods that use natural preservatives like vitamins C and E (tocopherols) to avoid potential problems. However, as mentioned earlier, simply because an artificial preservative isn't on the label doesn't mean it isn't present in the food. It just means that the pet food manufacturer didn't add any more.
- **Moisteners.** Moisteners like propylene glycol, the main ingredient in antifreeze, are added to "chewy" foods. Moisteners have no benefit and may be harmful to your dog.
- **Artificial flavors or colors.** Even though these have been shown to be safe, remember that your dog probably eats dog food every day. Most artificial colors haven't been tested that thoroughly.
- **Artificial sweeteners.** Artificial sweeteners include corn syrup, sucrose, and ammoniated glycyrrhizin. This stuff just makes bad food taste good.
- **Meat or poultry (or "animal") by-products of unknown origin.** Although some meat by-products (like liver) are fine, others really have no function other than to fill up the package. Because the label doesn't tell you exactly what's in the can or package, you're better off avoiding the whole crowd of them. (Many people also charge that by-products aren't handled as carefully as whole-meat products.) Whole meats are the way to go unless you

When large pet food companies perform palatability studies on their foods, they don't use Beagles for the testing. This is because Beagles eat anything with equal enthusiasm. Other dogs, though, show a definite preference for chicken.

know what the by-products are. On the other hand, good beef by-products like liver may be better for your dog than processed "meal." It really is a tough call.

- **Generic brands.** They are generally much lower in quality than named brands.
- **Generic meat.** Choose food with the specific name of a meat (like beef, chicken, or turkey) as the first ingredient. Foods that just say "meat" or "poultry" should be avoided. Unfortunately, just because a product has beef as the first ingredient doesn't mean that the product is mostly beef. Some companies engage in a practice known as "splitting." If they can possibly do so, they will divide the cereal products up into separate categories, like "rice" and then "brown rice." Added together, there may be more rice than beef. But because the manufacturers are allowed to list them separately, beef is listed first.

Dry Food (Kibble)

Most kibble is largely corn, rice, or soybean based. Better brands contain meat or fish as the first ingredient, and while they cost more, they are actually a better bargain because your dog doesn't need to eat as much of it. Kibble is also more calorie-dense than canned dog food, as canned food contains a lot more water by volume.

Canned Food

Although some canned dog food smells unpleasant to humans (one reason most people prefer to serve kibble), most dogs prefer both the aroma and flavor of canned foods. In fact, some people serve such unappetizing dry fare that they have to anoint it with canned food before their dogs will touch it.

To find the best canned food for your Beagle, check the label. Look for food containing whole meat, fish, or poultry as the first ingredient. Most lower quality canned foods have water as the first ingredient, and many canned foods are more than 78 percent water. The best canned foods use whole vegetables, not grain fractions like rice bran, rice flour, or brewers rice.

Unfortunately, the top canned foods can't often be found at the supermarket; you must go to the manufacturer, pet

Food stored improperly can become loaded with molds and other deadly toxins. To reduce the chances of your dog becoming a victim, be sure to use the freshest foods available. If you use a commercial food, check the manufacturing date. Do not buy in bulk—it may save you some money, but it's dangerous for your dog. Smaller bags get used more quickly and stay fresher longer.

stores, or dog shows. This is because the high cost of shelf rental space in most supermarkets is out of the reach of many small, premium pet food manufacturers.

Semi-Moist Food

There is a variety of food labeled "semi-moist" that comes in little packages. Most of this food looks good, but nearly all of it is bad for your dog. Semi-moist food is *loaded* with sugar in the form of corn syrup and beet pulp (up to 25 percent). It is also made up of about 50 percent water. Your dog does not need this stuff, which promotes obesity and tooth decay. The shelf life of these products is also lower than either canned or dry food.

Homecooked Meals and Raw Diets

One healthy alternative to commercial foods is a homecooked diet. In fact, it's quite possible to make a highly palatable, well-balanced meal for your dog at home. Of course, not every well-made homecooked meal will contain 100 percent of every nutrient your dog needs. It's also probable that not every single meal *you* eat will be "nutritionally balanced." Just follow the guidelines I list below and do your best.

A homecooked diet is a healthy alternative to commercial foods.

A good homemade diet can be more expensive than a cheap commercial dog food. This is especially true if you purchase human-grade, organically grown meat for your dog. But nutritionists who specialize in homemade diets say what you spend in the food market, you'll save at the vet.

Homemade food does not mean "table scraps," if you define that term as stuff that has gone bad and is ready to be thrown out. Bad food goes in the garbage. Good food goes in your dog. The best diets maintain nutritional balance by offering a rich variety of foodstuffs. Neither dogs nor humans need to have 100 percent of every nutrient in every meal. It's more important that both receive a diet high in variety and overall quality.

It is also true that preparing a healthy meal is more time consuming than plunking down a bowl of kibble. But there are ways to save time, such as cooking your dog's food at the same time you cook your own meals.

The greatest advantage of a homemade diet is that the power belongs to you, the dog owner. You control the ingredients. This is a great advantage for people who have dogs with health problems or multiple dogs with widely varying needs. If you decide to go the homemade route, be sure the diet provides the following:

- An animal-source protein. Unless your dog is allergic to all animal protein, a vegetarian diet is not normal and is not advised.
- A fat source, including essential fatty acids (EFAs).
- Adequate minerals, especially calcium, properly balanced with phosphorous.
- A supplement to provide vitamins and trace elements.

Many people feed their dogs raw food, and some claim it helps with allergies. This has not been my own experience. If you make your dog's food, cook it the same way you cook yours and for the same reasons: It's safer, it's more digestible, and it's more palatable. While most dogs can devour raw food and not become sick, in my opinion there's absolutely no point in taking the chance.

Treats

The simplest advice on treats that I can give is to go easy! The healthiest treats are bits of carrot or apple. You don't have to buy expensive biscuits filled with preservatives and dyes. For a special occasion, small chunks of cheese work perfectly.

Bones

Bones are naturally balanced sources of calcium and phosphorous, and dogs adore them. However, cooked bones

are dangerous, because they can easily splinter and damage your dog's throat and digestive system. The sterilized bones you can buy in the store are very dangerous in this regard: They are unnaturally hard and can cause broken teeth. Whole, *fresh* bones are safer, but the best choice is to have the bones thoroughly ground and cooked. Raw bones may carry bacterial dangers of their own, but the nutritional advantages are without par. It is important that the bones be both fresh and meaty for your dog to benefit. Start your dog off gradually, and watch him closely. Dogs need to learn to eat bones properly.

Your best choices are raw chicken legs and wings, because these bones have a perfect calcium/phosphorus ratio. Beef and even turkey bones may be too hard.

The most dangerous consequence of bone consumption is a perforated intestine, which allows toxins to escape into the dog's system. When dogs chew bones, they splinter, and splintering bones can puncture the esophagus or stomach. If you want to avoid these risks, give your Beagle some safe chew toys instead, such as Nylabones or rawhide chews.

For a special occasion, small chunks of cheese or beef are the perfect treat for your Beagle.

Substances to Avoid

Beagles will eat anything, including lots of stuff they shouldn't. It is in fact disconcertingly easy to poison a Beagle. Damage to the body is based on the amount of toxic substance ingested or inhaled, how big your Beagle is, and how long the substance is present in the body. Prompt treatment can result in a complete cure in many cases. If you suspect that your Beagle has been indulging in something bad, call your vet, even if the dog looks fine. Some poisons do not cause illness for days or even weeks after ingestion! Typical signs of poisoning include:

- Lethargy or sluggishness
- Vomiting
- Loss of appetite
- Staggering
- Breathing difficulty
- Seizure

In some cases, a Beagle could devour an object that, while not actually poisonous, could plug up the intestines. The best way for your vet to determine if an ingested object is causing problems is through an x-ray. The vet will look not only for the swallowed object itself, but also for abnormal amounts of gas in the intestine. If the x-ray is suspicious but not absolute, the vet may give your Beagle barium orally, which is like a white dye that coats everything in the stomach and intestine. The foreign object will appear white in the radiograph.

Grapes and Raisins

Reports have recently implicated large amounts of grapes and raisins (between 9 ounces and 2 pounds) in acute

Supplements

Many people believe that if a healthy dog is getting good food, supplements are not needed. This is usually true. The only problem is that even canine nutritionists are not completely sure what composes a good food. In addition, not all dogs are completely healthy, in which case it may make sense to add a little something extra to the diet.

Do not supplement minerals like calcium or phosphorous except at the direction of your veterinarian. Supplementing the carefully balanced minerals in your dog's food can lead to trouble. The same is true of certain fat-soluble vitamins like A and D; these vitamins are stored in the liver and can be toxic in large doses. (Vitamin E, another fat-soluble vitamin, does not appear to have toxic effects and may be supplemented if desired.)

Before you purchase a supplement, check out the source. Use a product that was designed for animals, even if it uses human-grade ingredients, as it should. The best supplements carry the Good Manufacturing Practices Certificate (GMP) and the ConsumerLab (CL) seal of approval. In addition, if the product has been produced according to the United States Pharmacopoeia (USP) guidelines, the label will say so. You should also look for organically grown herbs where possible.

kidney failure in dogs, although no one knows exactly why. The kidney shutdown is so dramatic that aggressive treatment may be necessary to save your dog's life. Treatment for animals who have been poisoned by grapes and raisins includes:

- Administering activated charcoal. This helps prevent absorption of the toxic substance, whatever it is.
- Blood tests to evaluate kidney function.
- Hospitalization with intravenous fluids.

Chocolate

Chocolate, especially baker's chocolate, can cause a range of problems, including cardiovascular difficulties and even seizures.

Onions

A quarter cup of onions can induce hemolytic anemia, a severe but usually temporary condition. Serious cases can even require a blood transfusion. Garlic has the same properties, but garlic in very small amounts probably does your dog some good.

Corncobs

Some people think it's interesting to watch their dogs deal with corncobs. It's not. Dogs are not horses, and the cobs can mortally impact the intestines.

OBESITY

You should be able to feel your Beagle's ribs easily without pressing, but you should not be able to *see* the ribs through the coat. There should be a "tuck-in" in the abdominal area. From above, your Beagle's figure should be shaped like an hourglass. A lean Beagle is not starving; rather, he is healthy. And studies show that not only do lean pets have fewer health problems, but they live on the average two years longer than their obese cousins.

Beagles are extremely prone to obesity, so you'll really need to monitor your dog. Remember that feeding guidelines on dog food bags and cans are a starting point only. (Following the directions on most of them will have you end up with an overweight Beagle.) Obesity is a contributing factor to many canine diseases, including

A healthy Beagle is well nourished and well hydrated.

diabetes, osteoarthritis, respiratory distress, liver disease, and heart disease. Once a dog comes down with one of these conditions, a vicious cycle sets in—a sick or arthritic dog can't exercise as much as a healthy one and so tends to gain even more weight.

Don't let your Beagle decide how much food he needs. Like most mammals, dogs are programmed to be hungry all the time. If given the opportunity, your Beagle will devour more than he needs to stay healthy. It's easier to keep him from getting fat in the first place than to try to take it off later on.

To help your dog lose weight and improve his cardiovascular system, start him on an exercise program, but establish a routine and begin gradually. It's not a bad idea to get him a health checkup first as well. Gradual conditioning will help strengthen his muscles, improve his flexibility, help his cardiac system, and even toughen his pawpads. Eventually, in the interest of cardiac health, your Beagle should get 20 to 30 minutes of aerobic exercise every day.

For weight loss, it doesn't matter. Four 10-minute sessions are just as beneficial as one 40-minute stretch.

If you're walking for exercise, let your Beagle take the first few minutes of the walk to snoop around and eliminate. Beagles like to run, but these scent-oriented dogs also enjoy sniffing around. Don't start the aerobic walking until your Beagle has had a chance to relieve him himself and do some smelling around. Make exercise sessions fun by including tag and fetch games—don't just stroll around the block. Make sure that you bring water so your Beagle won't get dehydrated.

A healthy Beagle is well nourished, well hydrated, and trim. The proper food in the proper amounts will ensure your Beagle leads a healthy, happy life. He'll thank you for it with many tail wags and lots of sweet Beagle kisses. Just don't let him kiss you right after he's eaten something strange.

If your Beagle is overweight, try him on this diet:
1/2 cup cooked lean meat
1/4 cup dry curd cottage cheese
1 cup cooked oatmeal
1/2 cup grated or chopped vegetables (leafy greens, broccoli, cauliflower, celery, and parsley)
1/2 cup bran
1 multivitamin supplement specified for dogs
Serve slightly warm.
You may also choose a high-fiber, reduced-calorie commercial diet, but check with your veterinarian first.

GROOMING
YOUR BEAGLE

Good grooming is about much more than good looks! It's about promoting good health, too. Grooming is not just a quick brushing and a rubdown. It includes nail, eye, ear, and dental care. In fact, every grooming session is actually a mini health exam, and it provides you with your best chance to notice lumps, bumps, infections, skin problems, breath odor, and other conditions that could signal disease. In addition, a good grooming session is like an extended petting. Your dog will thrive on it.

Beagles are clean dogs—at least, they are until they get dirty! Beagles have a medium length, smooth, "hard-lying" coat (meaning it lies close to the skin). Like most dogs, Beagles have a double coat comprised of a coarse outercoat and a soft undercoat. Beagles are shedders, and the shed cycle is tied into the length of day more closely than to the temperature. In any case, they will shed most in the spring. (A warm bath will sometimes speed up the process, but I always think this is a good time to take a vacation and let the boarding kennel deal with it.) Females in season may "blow their coats" after each heat. The great thing about Beagles, though, is that they are one of the easiest breeds to groom.

Your Beagle can get by with a few handy grooming supplies:
- Medium-bristled brush for brushing
- Hound mitt for polishing the coat
- A rake to remove the undercoat during a heavy shedding period
- Fine-toothed flea comb for extra-close removal of loose hair
- Mild shampoo
- A whitener for a stained coat
- Nail clippers
- Canine toothpaste

BRUSHING

Brush your Beagle with a medium-bristled brush or hound glove at least once a week. Apply the brush in long strokes along the body. This helps loosen dead hair so that it ends up on the brush rather than on your carpet. A fine-toothed flea comb will remove dirt and excess hair. Then, follow up with a hound glove to improve the shine of the coat. If some of the white part of the

Hound Odor

The average clean house Beagle does not have a strong hound odor, but if yours does, a bath once a week will solve the problem.

coat is discolored, you can use a whitener to remove the stain.

BATHING

Before you begin, get your equipment together. Start with a dog-safe shampoo, and include cotton balls for the ears and eye ointment to protect those tender eyes. If you do not want to get soaked yourself, get a waterproof apron. A spray attachment is also a necessity. To keep a recalcitrant dog in place, try a grooming noose; you can get one with a suction cup that attaches to the wall of the bath. Also, put a nonskid rubber mat on the floor of the bathtub. With a small Beagle, the kitchen or utility sink is the perfect place to bathe him. Otherwise, the bathtub is the next best place.

Bathing a dog is not very tricky, although it is important to wet him right down to the skin. Then, lather the dog all over with a mild soap. For the face, use a warm, damp washcloth and be careful not to let water get in the ears. After you've shampooed him, rinse the suds out thoroughly, and follow with a conditioning rinse if desired. Afterward, rinse the coat very carefully again. If soap residue is left in the hair, it can irritate your dog's skin. It will probably take *twice* as long to rinse the dog as it did to wash him. Then, towel dry him thoroughly, and don't forget to use plenty of towels. You can buy chamois-type towels that really soak up the moisture. If the coat is very thick, use a hand-held hair dryer on low or medium to dry him.

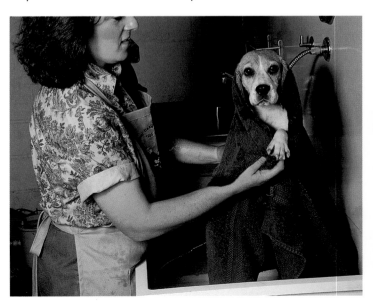

Beagles are one of the easiest breeds to groom.

After brushing your Beagle, use a hound glove to improve the shine of his coat.

Speak calmly or even sing to your Beagle while you're bathing him. He won't care if you're off-key; your pleasant voice will calm him. If your Beagle has seasonal allergies, bathe him regularly with a hypoallergenic shampoo in summer to remove allergens that adhere to the skin. If you need to use a medicated shampoo, make sure it stays on the dog for the allotted length of time. Contrary to myth, you can bathe your Beagle as often as you like if you use a mild shampoo and a good conditioner.

EYE CARE

Cleaning and examining the eyes should be a regular part of grooming. If a slight irritation appears, you can apply a commercial nonmedicated eyewash. Gently clean away any discharge that has gathered in the corners of the eye. If the discharge is yellow or green and the eye is swollen or red, the dog needs veterinary care immediately.

To examine your dog's eyes, simply stroke him gently on the head, pulling back the ears. The eyes will naturally open wider and come

The proper eye care includes gently cleaning away any discharge that has gathered in the corners of the eye.

clearly into view. A healthy dog's eyes should be wide open and bright. The center should be clear and shining, with pupils that are the same size. (If they are of unequal size, a neurological problem could be present.) The whites of the eyes should be pure white with no redness. Older dogs may have a greenish tinge to their eyes, but this is a normal characteristic of aging and nothing to worry about. The tissue beneath the lower lids should be a healthy pink, although some Beagles have a dark tinge on the membrane.

EAR CARE

Beagle ears require special attention, as they are prone to infection and infestation by ear mites. Clean them at least once a week. One easy way to check your Beagle's ear health is to smell those ears! Start by smelling them when you know they are clean and healthy. Foul or yeasty smells signal an infection, as does redness or irritation.

First, collect your materials, which should include cotton balls, paper towels, or moistened gauze sponges. Use a commercial ear cleaner or a combination of vinegar and water (if you can handle the smell). Vinegar does a good job of killing many varieties of fungus, but it's not an especially good cleaner, as it does not kill bacteria and is not especially good at removing debris from the ears. Avoid products that contain alcohol, because they sting.

Begin by cleaning the earlobe, removing the dirt, wax,

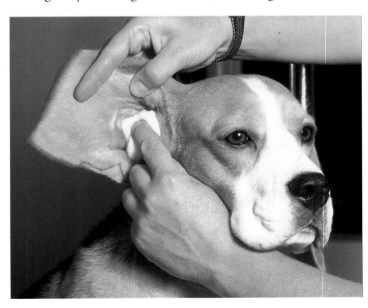

When cleaning your Beagle's ears, begin with the earlobe and then proceed to the cartilage.

and debris. Don't use cotton swabs; you're better off with thin wipes. (Thin wipes mold to your fingers better and work better to remove debris.) Then, proceed to the cartilage. The ear canal is shaped like an "L," so you will not be able to manually clean the entire ear; it's safest to just clean the parts you can see. Use a paper towel when you're finished to dry the ears; you do not want the dog to go running around shaking his head, as that can cause trauma to the inside of the ears. Repeat the procedure on the opposite ear. Then, give your Beagle a nice treat to reward him for his "pawfect" behavior.

NAIL CARE

If you can hear your dog's nails clicking on the floor, you know it's that time again. In fact, the nails should be even with the pawpad; anything hanging over should be clipped. Distasteful as it may be for your dog (and Beagles really dislike nail clipping), it's important for his health that his nails be kept at a reasonable length. You will have a much easier time with this procedure if you start doing it regularly while your dog is still a puppy. But even if your Beagle is grown when you get him, you can learn to trim his nails yourself. If you've never done it before, though, ask your vet or groomer to show you how the first time.

It's also important that you have the right instruments for the job—in this case, a nail trimmer specifically designed for dogs. If you choose clippers, you can use either pliers-type or guillotine-type clip-pers, whichever you prefer. I like the pliers type, myself. In either case, make sure they are sharp! Many peo-ple also like to use an electric nail grinder. And oddly, dogs seem to prefer them as well, once they get used to the noise. Be careful not to use them for too long a period, however, as they can heat up.

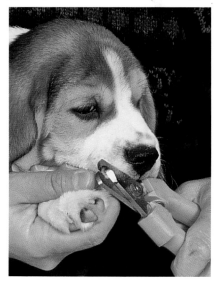

You will have to trim your Beagle's nails more often if he does not wear them down naturally on hard surfaces.

The frequency with which your Beagle's nails must be clipped depends on how much exercise he gets on hard surfaces, like pavement.

The key to successful nail trimming is to understand the anatomy of the nail. Look carefully at the nail. Inside the center or each nail is the "quick," or the blood and nerve supply. You don't want to cut into that! The quick is very easy to see in clear white nails. In black nails, where it is harder to see, you'll have to make several tiny cuts to reduce the chances of cutting into it. One of the great things is that the more you trim your Beagle's nails, the more the quick will withdraw back into the nail. This means there will be less of a chance that you'll cut into it the next time.

If you're lucky, you'll have one of those super Beagles who will sit in your lap while you clip the nails. Others may need to be restrained. In any case, cut the nail below the quick at a 45 degree angle. The cutting end of the nail clipper should be facing toward the end of the nail. If you accidentally cut into the quick, keep some silver nitrate on hand to stop the bleeding. You can get it at your pet supply store. If you don't happen to have that on hand, you can use cornstarch or flour. If the bleeding continues for more than 15 minutes, call your vet.

DENTAL CARE

Tooth brushing is as important for dogs as it is for human beings. More than 80 percent of all animals over two years of age have some kind of dental disease. Periodontal disease is one of the most common (and most preventable) diseases in both veterinary and human medicine.

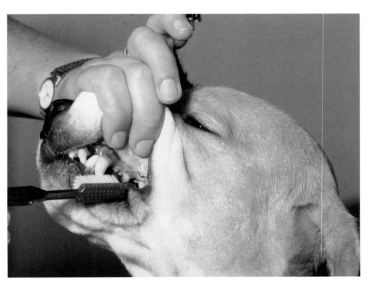

Brushing your Beagle's teeth will help remove the plaque and tartar that can cause periodontal disease.

You should begin dental care when your dog is a puppy, and brush his teeth every day. This may sound like a lot, but it only takes 30 seconds, really. Just the mechanical action of the brush helps remove plaque. If the plaque is not removed, it stays on the tooth and mineralizes, turning into the brown junk we call tartar. Both plaque and tartar are composed mostly of bacteria, and they can do a lot of damage to your Beagle's teeth. When brushing his teeth, you can use your own fingertip covered with gauze or a soft-bristled doggy toothbrush, which is pretty much the same thing as any other toothbrush. However, always use flavored canine toothpaste, available at pet supply stories. Dogs are not able to spit out toothpaste, and swallowing human toothpaste will lead to gastrointestinal trouble.

To get your dog used to the process, first accustom him to having you handle him around the mouth, lifting the lips, and so on. It helps if you have a little cheese or other tasty treat on your finger. Once you get him used to that, try rubbing his gums. Then you can progress to actually brushing. If your dog absolutely will not allow you to brush his teeth, you can use various gels and rinses designed to reduce dental disease. Rawhides and certain commercial diets may also help.

In addition to home care, it is important to get your Beagle's teeth checked out every six months by a vet. Depending on the individual care, professional cleaning may be required twice a year, or maybe only every three years.

ANAL SAC CARE

The anal sacs are two small glands just inside your pet's anus, packed with terrible-smelling secretions, whose purpose is not entirely understood. Wild animals can empty them on command to mark territory or for self-defense, but domestic dogs can't seem to do this. The sacs do usually empty when the dog defecates, but sometimes they become impacted, and you'll see the dog scoot around on his rear end. You can learn to empty the sacs by holding a tissue against the anus on each side and squeezing them. Sometimes it takes several tries. If an impacted anal sac is not emptied, it can form an abscess and rupture out through the skin. This situation calls for veterinary treatment and a course of antibiotics.

A swelling beneath the eye is a good indication of an abscessed carnassial tooth, a common condition in older dogs. If the tooth is not extracted, deadly bacteria can escape into the bloodstream and lodge in the heart.

If your dog continues to have trouble with his anal sacs, you can try switching him to a higher fiber diet. This produces a bulkier stool that may help empty the anal sacs when the dog defecates. In very severe cases, you might opt for an anal sacculectomy, a surgical procedure that permanently removes the sacs.

WINTER SKIN AND PAW CARE

Dry winter air outside and dry heat indoors can produce various skin conditions in Beagles. If you bathe your dog during the winter, use a soothing, oatmeal-based shampoo and follow with a moisturizer. Brush him frequently to help remove shed hair and keep the oils distributed throughout his body. In addition, feed your Beagle a high-quality diet that contains essential fatty acids.

Ice-melting products, typically composed of salt, can get lodged between your dog's toes, along with sand particles and ice crystals. These irritants are uncomfortable at best and dangerous at worst. They can cause painful cuts and cracked pawpads. After he has been outdoors, wash off his feet to remove ice and road salt. If your Beagle has a lot of hair between his toes, you may want to trim it. You can protect your dog's feet by putting petroleum jelly on the surface of the pads, or in serious cases, by using special booties made of neoprene, a type of synthetic rubber.

Brush your Beagle frequently during the winter months to help remove shed hair and distribute oils.

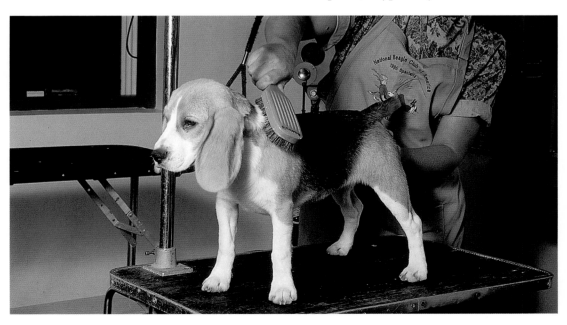

The Skunked Dog

Okay, your dog has been skunked! Now what? Well, here's what doesn't work: shampoos, perfumes, and colognes that mask but do not destroy the odor. That old folk remedy, tomato juice, doesn't work either, and you never have enough of the stuff in the house anyway. If you have to go out to buy something, buy something that works, like a commercial product specifically designed for skunk odor removal.

Most commercial products have one or more strategies to eliminate the odor. Some try to neutralize the smell by combining a couple of smells to create a third, more pleasant smell. Some try to bond the odor by changing the chemical structure of the actual odor particles. (This is usually only a temporary effect.) Others work by absorbing the odor; the active ingredient in the product actually swallows up the smell.

If you can't get to the store, try bathing the dog using a mixture of 1 quart of hydrogen peroxide, 1 cup of baking soda, and 1 teaspoon of a nice-smelling liquid soap. Then, rinse.

GROOMING FOR SHOW

Although the AKC standard declares that Beagles should be a "wear and tear" hound, you wouldn't know it from the efforts expended to shape them up a little for the show ring.

To do this right, you'll need to begin at least a month before the actual show (sometimes as long as three months if it's been a bad winter). Some people even hand-strip the dog, which means plucking out the heavy undercoat by hand. It's a long and laborious process, but it does make for a hard, glossy coat.

The rest of the grooming involves trimming away excess hairs, including the fuzz at the inner corner of the eyes (use thinning shears, a scissor with one solid and one serrated blade); the hairs around the edge of the ears; and the hairs around the upper lip. You can trim the neck with thinning shears, starting just below the ear, on line with the back edge of the skull, and trimming downward to the shoulder. You want to present a clean line. Use scissors to smooth the centerline over the front of the chest and also along the abdomen. If you have a male, the long hair over the genitals should be trimmed also. Use thinning shears to trim up the buttocks and base of the tail. Judges look for a smooth, convex line here. Trim away any fuzzy hair on the inside of the thighs. You can also trim the extra ragged hairs along the back of the front legs and pastern.

The tail should retain its brushy quality; to trim correctly, start scissoring in an upward line from just above the anus to about one-third the tail length. Don't square off the tip of the tail—it should be pointed.

Trim the extra hairs around the outside of the feet and between the pads. Show dogs are often trimmed back farther than pet dogs, although this is really not necessary.

TRAINING AND BEHAVIOR
OF YOUR BEAGLE

Some people give Beagles low marks for intelligence because these creative dogs are not robots or push-button obedience dogs. However, when Beagles are compared to several other breeds in practical and problem-solving abilities, they come out on top. Hounds of all kinds are independent thinkers, not automatons. To appreciate their wisdom, their humans need to be smarter than they are, and that's not always easy.

TRAINING ESSENTIALS

Today's Beagles lead tamer lives than their ancestors. Most never hunt rabbits, and to succeed in contemporary society, Beagles need to learn basic good manners and obedience training. However, training can still be an enjoyable experience for both you and your dog. One way to make it so is to keep lessons short—five or ten minutes is plenty of time. Another way is to pick a time when you are quiet and relaxed. It may help to have your Beagle burn off some of that extra energy first! Don't train when you're in a bad mood, either. You won't be effective, and your dog will sense your negative attitude.

Where to Train

Many experts believe that the best place to train your dog is in the kitchen. Most dogs have very positive feelings about kitchens, and positive feelings help reduce stress. However, if your dog has *overly* positive feelings about the kitchen, maybe you should select a more neutral spot. Whatever you choose, be sure to start indoors in a familiar place. The living room or recreation room may be good spots because they are generally large and familiar. Only when your Beagle responds perfectly inside should you take him outside. This is because the yard has too many distractions, and there's no way a dog treat can compete with the scent of a rabbit or the sight of a squirrel.

Think Like a Dog

Another essential training tool you should use is to think like a dog. This may sound diffi-cult, but it really isn't. That's because dogs think like people except that they are on a somewhat simpler level. They are motivated by the same things that motivate us: self-interest. They may

Only when your Beagle responds perfectly indoors should you take him outdoors to train.

not be as sophisticated as we are at marketing that self-interest, but the motivation remains. They want to know what's in it for them, which could be things like games, walks, praise, petting, and food.

Teaching a dog is really much more about teaching *ourselves* than it is about teaching Spot. The first lesson we need to teach ourselves is that of patience. Dogs learn by repetition, and they do not learn when they are yelled at. Beagles are particularly unresponsive to yelling. They either turn their ears off, or they become nervous. Neither response is what you want! If you become impatient and unhappy, the only message your dog will receive is that you are impatient and unhappy. He won't know why. But he'll probably conclude that danger is near (possibly to himself), and he'll become stressed. In a worst-case scenario, he'll

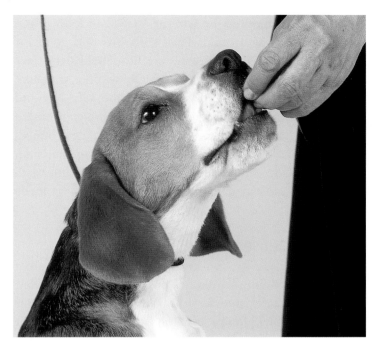

Food rewards should be given immediately after the desired action has been performed.

decide you are angry with him, and he will become scared. You dog should never, ever be afraid of you. A stressful environment is not conducive to learning or teaching.

Reward, Reward, Reward

Beagles in particular have a tremendous interest in food. That makes food a perfect reward for training. And reward is the key to good dog training. Dogs work better in hope for a reward than they do in fear of punishment. If a dog does something you like, he gets rewarded. If not, he doesn't. It's the simplest thing in the world. Forget wasteful, punitive, and cruel punishment-based training. These negative methods are not only cruel, they are not as successful as positive, reward-based training. However, in order for the food reward to be successful, it must be given promptly— within half a second of the action. The best food rewards are tasty and small (pea sized). In fact, you want a treat the dog can swallow right away, with no chewing needed.

Understand Your Beagle's Temperament

Be forewarned: Beagles can be stubborn. This is part of their beautiful hound nature. In the field it's called "persistence" or "independence," just the qualities you want in a hunting dog who is expected to be smart enough to find the game. Furthermore, he will expect you to follow him, not the other way around. This is all well and good for hunting dogs, but when Beagles are household pets, their independent natures can pose something of a problem, especially to an owner so beguiled by the soft eyes and tender expression of this breed that she is completely misled about its true character: stubborn, willful, determined, independent, obstinate, unyielding, uncompromising, strong willed, bullheaded, muleheaded, pigheaded, intractable, headstrong, and tenacious. I hope I have made myself clear.

Channel a Sense of Play

Because Beagles are fun-loving dogs, it makes sense that good Beagle teaching should rely on a Beagle's sense of play. To do this, include games in your training sessions. Let your dog play a quick round of hide-and-seek for food, for instance. Even running around the room letting your dog

Including games in your training sessions will help keep your Beagle from becoming bored.

chase you is a great tension reliever. (Don't chase him, though; this will only show him it's okay to run away from you, and that you'll follow.)

Unfortunately, a lot of dog teaching advice is written for Labrador Retrievers, Border Collies, and other workaholic breeds. What works for them won't necessarily work for Beagles. Beagles are dogs who are particularly interested in their physical environment; they are much more closely attuned to the smells and sounds of the woods than they are to you. This is part of their hunting heritage: They were bred to be independent searchers of game. To make your dog pay more attention to you than he does to anything else is a challenge. You have to provide him with a reason for listening.

Use Appropriate Eye Contact

One of the most important visual messages is transmitted through eye contact. In the dog world, dogs avoid gazing at each other unless issuing a challenge. Modern dogs have learned that our looking into their eyes is probably not meant as a prelude to an attack, but a prolonged stare will make most dogs nervous. Very dominant or aggressive dogs might stare back—and then bite you. It's usually better just to look at the tip of a dog's ear unless he's very comfortable with you staring at him.

SOCIALIZATION

Beagles are naturally sociable creature. They like everybody, including the elderly, children, and other dogs. This is probably the world's least aggressive breed. Still, socialization is important, not to prevent your dog from becoming aggressive, but to help him develop a sense of confidence. Certain lines of Beagles appear to have genetically-based shyness. Getting your Beagle out and about and meeting lots of folks in lots of situations will help him develop into a secure and confident dog. In fact, if you have a puppy or undersocialized dog, try to expose him to 100 new people and many different positive situations within four months.

HOUSETRAINING

Beagles are rather famous for being slow to housetrain. And while your Beagle might learn it all in four or five days,

Cleaning up is an important part of good housetraining. You might not be able to smell those lingering odors in the house, but your Beagle sure can. You absolutely must clean all spots where your Beagle has eliminated indoors. Whatever commercial or homemade preparation you decide to use, don't use ammonia to clean the area, because it smells just like urine to a dog.

don't be alarmed if it takes longer. That is normal with this breed, and is, I am afraid, one reason why so many Beagles end up being outdoor dogs. This need not happen with some patience on your part.

The basic rules for housetraining are pretty simple, and you should begin the process the first day you bring home your new Beagle. When you are home with your dog, supervise him. You might even keep a 10-foot leash on him and tether it to yourself via your belt. Observe him for signs of discomfort, and take him out immediately. (Signs may include whining, sniffling, circling, trying to hide, yawning, or flicking his tongue.) The main thing to remember is that when your Beagle needs to go out, you need to take him out, even if it is three o'clock in the morning. This is the only way you will ever get your dog housetrained.

When taking your Beagle outside, lead him to the same spot each time. The smell of previous eliminatory activity will signal to him what he is supposed to do next. *Go with your dog*—don't just abandon him to the yard. First, you want to actually observe his success and praise him, and second, if you don't go with him, he will think that showing he has to eliminate will result in banishment. Oh, he'll still eliminate all right, but it will be in the house, and he just won't tell you about it.

Don't rush the housetraining process. It may take a month or more before your dog is reliably housetrained, and puppies don't have complete bowel and bladder control until they're about nine months of age.

Treats

Beagles enjoy treats, so you might want to give him a tiny, pea-sized treat if he successfully eliminates outdoors. Bring the treat outside with you or keep some in your coat pocket. Don't be in a hurry to go back inside, because puppies often eliminate more than once. If he doesn't accomplish anything in ten minutes, take him back in for about a minute and then go out and try again. Odds are you'll be successful the second time. If it still doesn't work, do the in and back out thing until it does. And when he's done, don't hasten him back in the house. Let him walk or play. If he gets the idea that the minute he eliminates he has to go back in the boring house, he'll try to hold it as long as possible. That's not fun

for either of you. A combination of play, treats, and praise is enough to convince most Beagles that housetraining is a great adventure.

Because Beagles enjoy food so much, try rewarding him for successfully eliminating outdoors with a treat.

Scheduling

The more watchful and observant you are, the more quickly you will housetrain your Beagle. Puppies usually need to eliminate after they eat, drink, chew on a toy, play vigorously, and after they wake up from a nap. Pretty much all the time, in other words. Remember, they have tiny little bladders and not very good sphincter control. That's why scheduling regular feeding and walking times is so important. Feed and walk your Beagle at the same time every day. Dogs really hate unpredictability, and a dog who is continually exposed to a routineless existence will become shy and less confident.

Confinement

When you are away from home, confine your dog to safe, tiled area like the bathroom, kitchen, or his crate. Give him something to play with while he's in there, like a good chew toy, for instance. Don't leave him alone in the crate any longer than you can reasonably expect him to hold it, which is no more than a couple of hours for a young puppy. If possible, hire a pet walker to help out.

Beagles are very different from many other dogs about their sleeping quarters. In fact, Beagles in some circles do the unthinkable—they actually mark their sleeping quarters by urinating on them. This is not common in other breeds, although it is apparently common protocol among some Beagles. The only way out of this is to hope it happens just once, or you might try placing the blankets marked with his scent inside the crate. This may prevent him from urinating on them in the future.

Accidents

If an accident does occur, clean it up promptly without reacting to it. You should never yell at your Beagle, hit him, or rub his nose in it. If you actually catch him in the act, clap your hands to startle him, and scoop him up with his tail between his legs. Say, "Out!" in an excited but not angry voice. Reward him for doing the right thing when he does eliminate outdoors.

PUPPY KINDERGARTEN AND DOG OBEDIENCE SCHOOL

Puppy kindergarten provides your Beagle puppy an opportunity to have fun with other youngsters in a friendly and relaxed environment. And you'll meet lots of fellow dog lovers, too! Just as important, your puppy will not only learn some basic commands, but he'll get practice going out for trips and learning to ride in the car. Because some Beagles tend toward shyness, this is a great way to help them develop some confidence.

When considering a training course, make sure you choose the right teacher. Not everyone understands the unique Beagle mentality, and some have the erroneous idea that Beagles are difficult (or impossible) to train. This is because many of them do most of their work with Labradors and Golden Retrievers, dogs who stand around waiting to be told what to do. Beagles are a whole different school of fish, so to speak. Don't be afraid to ask questions before you begin the training course. Some questions you may want to ask include:

- What is the instructor's formal education or experience? The best trainers don't necessarily need a degree in applied animal behavior, but it doesn't hurt to have one, either.
- What is the instructor's method of teaching? Does she rely on choke chains, force, or negative reinforcement, or does she advocate kind, positive training with lots of rewards? (This latter type is the only one for a Beagle!)
- To what professional organizations does the trainer belong? One of my favorites is the Association of Pet Dog Trainers, an organization that advocates and specializes in nonviolent, positive training methods.
- Does the trainer provide structured "homework?" Does she give out written handouts and summaries? Is she available for consultation? A trainer who does all of these things is ideal, although many good trainers may only do one or two of these things.

Be sure you know what you want your dog to get out of class. Most Beagles are not candidates for obedience titles, although it can be done. It's more reasonable to choose a class that emphasizes basic skills in a fun atmosphere. If your Beagle turns out to be that rare obedience natural, you can move up to a different class.

Choose a professional trainer who understands your Beagle's unique personality.

BASIC TRAINING

Basic commands are best taught in a fun, secure, game-like environment. Not all Beagles are equally biddable. To learn if yours is, here's a quick test. Does your Beagle seem responsive to your moods? Does he appear sad or upset when you are? If so, he's probably a responsive dog who will learn quickly, if only because he wants to please you. Less biddable dogs are trainable, too, of course. You will just have to be freer with the treats.

And speaking of treats—you will need to use treats to train your food-oriented Beagle, but these don't have to be high-calorie items like cheese or even dog biscuits. Try healthy and inexpensive treats, like small bits of apple or carrot. Avoid grapes or raisins, however, as some dogs have been severely affected by an unknown toxin they contain.

Often we think that the basics of training are the words themselves, like sit, come, or stay. However, many dogs respond better to visual cues and rewards. For example, if you say, "Let's go for a run" and your dog responds with

Looking for a professional trainer? The Association of Pet Dog Trainers is an excellent place to start. This organization was founded for trainers and pet owners alike.

Small, healthy treats provide the perfect food reward during basic training exercises.

unbridled enthusiasm, it just might be because he's noticed you glancing toward the door and eyeing his leash. Beagles are alert to even the smallest gestures. As for your voice, its tone is just as important as the words you say, probably more so. If you say in a sweet, happy tone, "Oh, you awful little Beagle, what a terrible bad boy you are!" he will probably wag his tail happily.

The following are the fundamentals of obedience that all Beagles should know. Remember to speak in a crisp, cheerful determined voice during training sessions, and be happy but firm. Use short words for commands, because they are quicker for you to say and easier for the dog to remember, and always end your training sessions on a positive note. You can accomplish this by asking your dog to do something he likes and at which he will always succeed. Then, reward him!

Come

Begin with your Beagle on an 18- or 20-inch rope. Let him wander off, and then call him to you while saying the command in an excited, happy voice: "Come!" If he comes, give him a small treat or some affection; if he doesn't come, then gently pull him to you and reward him when he gets to you. Practice this for five minutes at the most. You can even try using a whistle.

Most Beagles respond better to a whistle than to voice or hand commands. Get yourself a stainless steel "referee" whistle with a lanyard attached. The classic whistle command for a Beagle is three sharp blows on the whistle for the come command. This is a very loud sound that can carry a mile in fall and winter. To train your Beagle to come using a whistle, start in a small area and bring your bag of treats. Sit right down in front of the pup and blow the whistle three times softly. Then, hand over a treat. This is basically the same method as clicker training, but Beagles tend to run too far to hear the sound of a clicker. Anyway, do this a few times, and then go play. Repeat a couple of hours later, and stand farther away from him. Soon, he'll associate the sound of the whistle with you, petting, and treats. A word of warning, though—this will not work if your Beagle has found a rabbit. Nothing will.

Whoa!

This emergency field command is a lifesaver. Its purpose is to get your Beagle to stop whatever he's doing immediately. It's most useful when your Beagle has escaped from the house and is headed directly into the street. Calling, "Come" might tell your Beagle that you want him home, but he's apt to make a large circle while doing so—right into the traffic. Saying, "Whoa!" tells him to stop at once. Once he halts, you can walk over to him and snap on the leash.

To begin teaching, you need a plain collar (not a choke chain), a leash, and a long line. Start with the regular lead. While he is standing still (as you want him to), say, "Whoa!" Then, praise or treat him, but keep him standing. After a short period of praise, say, "Release!" and play (but don't run) with him. Then, try again. Soon he should associate "whoa!" with standing still and receiving a treat. As time goes on, use the long line instead of the regular leash. This allows you more distance but also more control. If he doesn't respond to "whoa!", stop him with the lead. When he stops, praise and treat him, or play with him some more. It's very important that his reward is not a run. You want to connect the whole procedure of stopping and staying with praise and food. When he stops reliably on a lead, you can try him off lead. Use your backyard or some other boring, fenced area for starters.

If you have done a good, thorough job with "whoa!", you just might save your Beagle's life. You can never absolutely count on a dog obeying your commands, however, so even with an apparently completely obedient Beagle, it's not wise to allow him off lead in the hopes that "whoa!" will automatically save him if he runs into traffic. A five- or ten-minute training session is sufficient.

Leave It

This simple command is also a lifesaver. Dogs are forever getting into garbage and poisons, not to mention your own dinner. Start teaching him by waiting until he is chewing on an object that he really doesn't care *that* much about. (It should also be one that's not important to you, either, of course.) As he's chewing, go up to your dog, and say, "Leave it!"

Offer him a treat in exchange. Practice several times a day, and always offer the dog a treat that he likes better (like bacon) than whatever he is chewing. You want to reinforce that he'll be richly rewarded, not given a mere sop like a dog biscuit.

In real life, you would be most likely to use this command when your dog has gotten into something truly heady like a chicken carcass, so your established reward needs to be very powerful. Of course, you probably won't have any bacon actually on hand when the chicken carcass event occurs, but it's okay to cheat that one time and just reward him with a biscuit. Afterward, practice the leave it command several more times with your accustomed treat and plenty of praise.

Off

The funny thing about Beagles is that they always tend to be on something when you want them off. The answer is not necessarily disallowing the privilege of furniture but teaching them a positive rather than a negative command. Say, "Off!" in a cheerful voice and lure your dog with a treat and praise. Of course, if you never want him on that piece

Teaching your Beagle the off command is a great way to keep him off your favorite furniture.

of furniture, you can use your dark growly voice, but if you just want to move him temporarily, the off command works very well.

Wait

This calming command is useful when you have company. Your dog doesn't have to sit, which can be very trying when friends have arrived. Instead, he should merely stand quietly and wait to be petted. It's also useful for you to keep your dog from charging for the door while you are headed to open it, either to let someone in or to go out yourself.

To teach the wait command, begin by attaching a short leash to your Beagle. This will serve to give you a little control. Touch your Beagle quietly on the rump and say, "Wait" when a visitor arrives. Use the leash to restrain him if you have to, and reward him for quietly waiting to be petted.

Sit

Sit is an easy command to teach, but it is often used inappropriately—usually when the owner really wants the dog to stay still, get out of the way, or not make a nuisance of himself. The catch-all phrase "sit, boy" is supposed to magically cure all the bad habits your dog has established. It doesn't of course, and it's much better to work on actually

When your Beagle successfully completes the sit command, praise him and give him a treat while he's still sitting.

curing your dog's bad habits (like jumping up) than to tell him to sit every time he does them. Think of it this way: Most of the time, when you ask your dog to sit, you really would be happy if he just stood there quietly. If that's what you want, that's what you must teach him. Sit is a useful command, of course. I ask my dogs to sit before I give them a treat, because it's easier for me to find their little mouths that way. It's useful as a prelude to nail clipping. And it's a simple trick for children to practice with the family dog. But it's no substitute for good all-around behavior.

The easiest way to teach the sit is to say, "Sit" in a cheerful voice while holding a treat over his head. Then, gently start curving the treat backward over the dog's head. Most dogs will sit naturally. Praise him and give him the treat. In the few cases where this doesn't work, you may press very gently down on the Beagle's backside, saying, "Sit." Do not force him to do this; encourage him. Nothing about the training should be uncomfortable. When your Beagle succeeds, praise him softly, and while he is still sitting, give him a treat. If he gets up too quickly, refrain from treating him. He needs to learn that the treat comes only when he is actually sitting. Otherwise, you'll turn him into a jack-in-the-box.

Stay

Although some people teach the stay as a separate command, I prefer to use the sit, which means that my dog should sit until I say, "Okay!" I believe that teaching the stay as a separate command is confusing to dogs, because you're not asking them to do anything new—you're just asking them to keep doing what you have already asked them to do. However, other people believe that saying, "Stay" signals to the dog early that he'll be sitting for quite some time. At any rate, never ask your dog to sit-stay for more than a few seconds when you are starting out. You want to make success easy for him.

Teach stay by saying the word and slowly retreating. Reward him for remaining in one place. Again, quit while the training is still fun. The length of time you teach this command depends on your individual dog, but five minutes is usually long enough.

Down

Most dogs dislike being asked to lie down, although they are happy enough to do it on their own. This is because "down" puts them in a physically and psychologically vulnerable position.

To teach down, use the treat method again. While the dog is sitting, lower the treat slowly and move it toward the floor. Most dogs will lie down naturally. If yours doesn't after a few tries, you can gently extend his front legs and praise him as you ease him to the floor. Don't push down on your Beagle's shoulders to force him down; you can actually dislocate his shoulder in trying to coerce a stubborn Beagle. Remember, you want him to perform joyfully, not out of fear or pain. Keep the length of your training sessions short, preferably about five minutes.

Heel

Your leash is your dog's best friend, as well as a necessary tool. Don't think of the leash as a restraining device; think of it as a way to stay close to your dog. With only a little encouragement, your Beagle will look forward happily to the sight of the leash being taken off its hook, because it means walk time!

Because Beagles are rather small dogs, you'd think it would be a cinch to teach them to walk calmly on a lead. And it's really not very hard, although you'd never know it by the alarmingly large number of Beagle owners you see permanently entangled by their own leashes, while their Beagles dart merrily all around them.

Before you start leash training your Beagle, give him a lot of free exercise. A somewhat tired dog will be more amenable to moving at a slow pace. Beagles like to go first. Remember that they are bred to be leaders on a hunt. To some extent, you are working against Beagle nature when you are asking him to follow you. You must replace his natural hunting instinct with an equally natural instinct of "follow the leader." When he becomes convinced that *you* are the leader and that you know where the "pack" is supposed to go, he'll be more willing to follow.

Begin working with your Beagle when he is on a lead, not free. He should be responding to the come command before you start teaching him to heel (which means to walk nicely on a lead at your heel). Enforce your command if necessary by kneeling and using a treat to lure him. Don't pull on the leash. Only use it to keep him from going in the other direction. Also, walk fast, at least at first. This will keep his attention directed straight ahead, where you want it while training.

It is customary to have the dog walk on your left side, so if you plan to engage in formal obedience training, you might as well start with the correct practice right away. Start by keeping a little treat in your left hand. The point is to get the Beagle to believe that staying close to that appendage is likely to yield rewards. Because a Beagle is pretty low to the ground, however, bend down when you feed him. You don't want to get him in the habit of jumping up for the treat.

Treat your dog frequently as you walk along, but only when he's in the correct heel position. To help position your dog, hold the leash behind your thigh. Start walking in a counterclockwise circle. Because your dog will be on the inside, you'll find it easier to guide him as you move along. Say, "Trooper, heel!" in a bright voice and start walking. Don't scold him if he goes in the wrong direction—just don't respond to it. Stay still or move in a different direction. Soon, he'll realize that all the rewards come from staying near you.

After your Beagle becomes accustomed to walking on the leash and you don't have to give him a treat every two seconds for walking politely, ask him to sit when you stop. Reward him when he does. Soon your Beagle will sit calmly by your side whenever you stop to chat with friends. If you do not want your Beagle to sit automatically at every stop, make sure you say, "Sit" before you give him a treat.

Don't make every walk a lesson. Allow your Beagle plenty of time to snoop around and check things out, especially when you begin your walk. It may be exasperating to you, but Beagles really enjoy this part of the adventure. You can signal to your Beagle that a certain part of the walk is his turn to lead by using some special command (whatever you like) and loosening up on the lead. I say, "You lead!" and start following him. This is very important also if you plan to participate in tracking with your Beagle.

For inveterate pullers, or if you have untrustworthy small children, purchase the Wayne Hightower harness. It is simple, dogs love it, and it works better than anything else I have seen, including head halters.

PROBLEM BEHAVIORS

The first thing to remember about a problem behavior is that for *you* it's a problem. For the dog, it's a *reaction* to a completely different problem that he is experiencing. For example, let's say a dog is lonely or bored. That is his problem. His solution might be to chew something, which you see as the problem. However, this action happens to relieve his tension, and it provides him with something to do. It's a fact that every "problem" dog behavior is, for the dog, a *solution* to a problem.

Fortunately, there are some adjustments that you can make that will help you and your dog live together in harmony:

1. **Change your behavior.** It may be that you are doing something, consciously or unconsciously, to produce the behavior you are trying to correct. For example, cuddling a frightened dog is guaranteed to reinforce the fearful behavior. It's easier to train yourself than to train your dog, anyway.
2. **Change your dog's behavior.** This may include teaching him to accept baths, obey basic commands, release toys and food, and so forth. Naturally, to get your dog to behave differently, you will probably have to do something different yourself.
3. **Build a higher fence, confine the dog, etc.** Some canine behaviors are so ingrained that it may be impossible to train the dog out of them. If you can't retrain, you must restrain.
4. **Medicate the dog.** Some bad behavior has a medical cause. If this is the case, it may have a medical solution.
5. **Medicate yourself.** Perhaps a nice cup of herbal tea will put you in a better temper.
6. **Get used to it.** This seems a bit harsh, but sometimes it's easier for everyone concerned. If your dog has a minor problem behavior that doesn't lend itself to any of the above treatments, just ignore it.

One size does not fit all. The cure that works depends on the target behavior, its cause, and your patience. The important thing to remember is that most inappropriate dog behaviors are "fixable." Consistent training (routines are great!), fair leadership, and patience are the keys. As leader, you are the one to make the decisions, control the resources (like food and attention), and set the boundaries. It's mostly common sense, especially if you stop once in a while to think, "How does my dog perceive what I am doing?"

Let's look at a few of the more common problems Beagle owners may face and at least some of the ways to deal with them.

Chewing

Most dog chewing is normal, although inconvenient. Dogs chew because they are dogs. They don't do it to spite you but may resort to it if they are bored or lonely. For you, it's a problem, but for your Beagle, it's a sensible way to release energy and comfort himself.

To prevent your dog from chewing on your valuable possessions, provide him with appropriate chew toys instead.

Solution

If you are nervous about your dog chewing your belongings while you are gone, don't let him have access to them. Instead, provide him with plenty of acceptable things to chew on. Stuff hard, hollow toys with treats or give him a big, tough rawhide. Stay away from dried or sterilized bones. Many of these are harder than tooth enamel and in fact are the most common cause of tooth breakage in dogs. The same is true for cow hooves. If you and your dog are outside, try burying the toys in a special digging pit you've made just for him. If your Beagle doesn't seem to enjoy toys, you may have to "teach" him to use them by playing with him and them at the same time.

Copraphagia (Stool Eating)

The Beagle's tastes extend far beyond what many consider food. Sometimes they eat feces—either their own or that of another dog or cat. Contrary to common belief, stool eating doesn't mean the dog has worms or is not eating a nutritionally balanced diet.

Solution

To curb this habit, simply keep the yard picked up. It may also help to feed your Beagle more frequently (but not a greater amount) to help reduce his appetite. A high fiber diet, which will make the dog feel fuller, may also help. Keep your Beagle busy, too. Bored dogs are more likely to take up this repulsive habit. And if all else fails, you can buy certain products to put in your dog's food that make his own feces unpalatable to him.

Digging

Beagles have good reasons for turning your yard into a minefield, even though the reasons may not be apparent to you:

- He could be hot. (Digging down into the soft, cool soil is both entertaining and refreshing.)
- He could be bored. (He may feel the need to do something to while away the empty hours. Also, Beagles don't like to be left alone.)
- He may be giving way to predatory instincts. (There are a lot of moles and other underground prey scampering just below the earth's surface.)
- He may be trying to escape. (This can be a combination of wanderlust, boredom, loneliness, and predatory instinct—all the good game is outside the fence.)
- She may be pregnant. (You're looking at normal nesting behavior.)
- He may be having fun. (Lots of dogs enjoy digging, especially in soft earth just for the fun of it, the way kids will play in a sandbox.)

Solution

The solution to digging partly depends on the cause. If your Beagle is hot, bring him inside where it's cool. If your Beagle is bored or lonely, entertain him, exercise him, and give him more of your company. Most people seriously underexercise their dogs. If he is trying to escape, make sure he can't. In some cases, this will require installing some cement below the fence line. If he is following predatory instincts, you'll have to either keep a close eye on him or simply take him in the house. If she is pregnant, find her a suitable whelping box. And if he is digging for the pure pleasure of it, install a sandbox full of fresh, soft earth in an appropriate place in your yard, and encourage him to dig there by loading it up with hidden bits of food and special

Burying Bones

Everyone knows that dogs bury bones, but not everyone knows why. The reason lies deep within the canine collective memory. When dogs were wolves, no one could be sure of getting a meal every day. The smartest thing to do then was to hide or cache leftovers from other members of the pack. Bones are filled with nutritious marrow and work well to tide one over during hungry times. So even though your pet dog is well fed, his genetic heritage may compel him to hide bits of his dinner in the yard, under the sofa, or even behind the pillows.

toys. Play there yourself until he gets the idea, and spray forbidden areas with a dog repellent. There are plenty of them on the market. By the way, if you are fertilizing your lawn with bone or blood meal, the scent could be fooling your dog into believing there's something really good buried in your yard.

Separation Anxiety

Separation anxiety is a self-perpetuating condition that occurs in response to being left alone. It manifests itself in panting, howling, abnormal drooling, barking, and destructive chewing. It does no good to chastise a dog with this condition, because he's really not in control of his actions. Experts believe that the condition is caused by overstimulation of the parts of the brain that regulate fear and stress responses.

Separation anxiety is a common condition in rescued Beagles; in fact, it is most frequently seen in shelter or rescue dogs. These animals have already had a horrible experience with abandonment.

Solution

In dogs with separation anxiety, it turns out that most destructive chewing occurs right after the owner leaves and just before he returns home, when the dog's anxiety level is highest. To avert the first, leave some chew toys around. By

Separation anxiety is a condition that occurs in response to being left alone.

the time he's done with them, he may be relaxed enough to stop chewing, at least for a few hours. To avert the second scenario, some owners teach their dogs not to greet them and to bring them a chew toy instead. They do not greet the dog until he presents the toy. Within a few days, the dog figures out that it's a good idea to have a toy on hand in anticipation of the owner's return. As anxiety builds as the magic hour draws near, he begins to chew nervously on the toy rather than on the furniture.

Because Beagles are pack dogs, they may be comforted by the addition of another dog or even a cat, but don't count on it. (And don't get another pet merely in the hope that he will cure your dog's anxiety.) It's human companionship they crave, as a rule. But more than other breeds, Beagles can frequently be helped by the addition of a fellow pet.

Today, a medication called Anipryl has been approved for use in treatment of separation anxiety. It is most effective when used along with desensitization therapy. This involves having the owner leave for a very short period of time (like a minute) and then gradually, over several weeks, increasing the length of time away.

In some cases in which a dog regards his crate as a comforting den, crating a dog may be helpful, although I believe that most people who crate dogs crate them for too long. However, many dogs with separation anxiety also have barrier anxiety and go completely bonkers in a crate. It largely depends on whether or not your dog has had previous bad experiences with crates.

Separation Anxiety…or Something Else?

Not all misbehavior that occurs when you're gone is real separation anxiety. The condition is often misdiagnosed. Much destructive behavior simply occurs because the dog is bored and decides to destroy an object just for something to do. After all, dogs don't have stamp collections, and Beagles were bred to be working dogs, with plenty of company around and lots to do all day long. Dogs with real separation anxiety will chew really strange things (like linoleum) that they wouldn't normally pay attention to. They also will chew things that are close to exit points, or things that belong to their owners. Some may howl or eliminate inappropriately. Merely bored dogs won't, unless you're gone so long that they can't "hold it." In addition, dogs with true separation anxiety will begin the destructive behavior, howling, or inappropriate elimination within a few minutes after you leave and in some cases even before. The destructive chewing that results from boredom won't begin until the dog actually becomes bored.

Many dogs jump up because they were never discouraged from doing so as puppies.

Jumping Up

Many dogs jump up because we have taught them that that is what we want. If your Beagle never received encouragement for doing this as a puppy, he wouldn't be doing it now. However, it's never too late to make a change, though it does require an unwavering consistency on the part of you and your guests to make it work.

Solution

The best way to get your dog to stop jumping up is to not reward that behavior—not with a look or sound. When your dog jumps up, fold your arms and look away. Do not respond. If he continues, just walk away. Don't look at him. In fact, ignore him completely. When he ceases jumping up, immediately get down to his level and reward him with praise and attention. After a week or so, he will get the idea. The key is to make sure everyone understands that this is the treatment. Only then, with consistent effort, will it work.

Barking

Barking is a natural behavior, but with Beagles it can be too much of a good thing. In fact, Beagles consistently rank at or near the top of the "barking breeds" list. While it's nice to know that your Beagle will warn you of trespassers, strange-looking birds, and a twig falling in the yard, sometimes it can be somewhat annoying, especially to the neighbors.

Of course, sometimes they may bark for no reason, just as people talk for no reason. Most of the time, however, dogs know very well why they are barking. And because communication is by definition a two-way street, dogs also glean tons of information about other dogs from their barks. They know how far away the barker is and in what direction. They know how excited or sad or angry he is. (Loudness, pitch, and rate are good indicators of these things.)

Solution

If your dog barks to warn you of visitors, that's fine. Praise him for the barking, and reassure him that all is well. If he continues to bark, ignore him until he stops. If your dog is barking to request something like treats or going for a run, deny the privilege until the dog ceases to bark, and then reward quiet behavior. If your Beagle is barking because he's excited to be outside, bring him in the second he starts. He'll soon learn that barking results in being brought back into the house.

Phobias

Dogs have recognized phobias, just as people do. Documented types include fear of thunder, firecrackers, gunshots, car travel, other dogs, odors, and certain people.

Solution

The best way to address a phobia is to desensitize and countercondition the dog to the feared object or event. This simply means to get the dog to associate the feared object or event with good things rather than bad things. For example, teach your Beagle to down-stay for a food reward. Give the reward if the dog shows no fear response (panting, digging, pacing, etc). In the case of thunderphobia, you can try playing a recording of a thunderstorm, but many dogs won't respond to a recording in the same way that they will to the actual event, which is composed of more than noise. Don't coddle the dog, as that will convince him there is something really wrong. Drug therapy is also useful in some cases; consult your vet for more information.

Shyness

Shyness is an inherited trait in some families of Beagles. It is not desirable but has often been allowed to remain because that particular line of dogs was superior in other ways. In fact, among some hunting Beagles, certain shy Beagles continued to be bred because they could run the hair off a rabbit. This was a mistake, because these same shy Beagles became impossible to catch once the hunt was over!

Solution

Shyness is extremely common in some lines of Beagles, and experts agree there is a genetic component involved. The same thing seems to be true in human beings—it all has to do with the amygdala structures in the brain. This means that a genetically shy Beagle cannot be trained out of being shy. However, careful socialization and proper training will help a shy dog become less shy. In fact, you can help your dog become more confident by exposing him to a multitude of positive experiences, including a fun puppy kindergarten or training class. Try walking your Beagle on a different path every day, and if he seems nervous, try jogging with him to distract him.

Play with your dog a lot, letting him chase you. Crawl around on the floor at his level, and even try covering your face and making high-pitched, puppy-like noises. Avoid eye contact, which to dogs can be threatening. As your Beagle becomes less shy, try playing tug-of-war, and allow him to win often.

If you have other dogs, don't allow them to stare at your shy dog while he's eating or trying to sleep. Give him a place of his own. A shy dog will also gain confidence if you sit down on the floor next to him, rather than towering above him.

Never coddle your shy dog—this just convinces him that something is really wrong. Also, it's important to be calm, relaxed and nonstressed yourself. Some of that will wear off on your Beagle. Most importantly, never use any form of punishment on a shy dog.

Dominance and Aggression

Only rarely do Beagles exhibit this distasteful behavior, but when they do, it's always serious and needs to be addressed. If your Beagle has ever bitten you (other than a misplaced nip when he was a puppy), you should talk to your vet and have a medical workup done. The vet may also be able to recommend a behaviorist.

One of the scariest early signs of aggression is a growl. However, a growl may not mean that your dog is about to tear you limb from limb. It's a form of communication like any other. Generally, it means "Back off!" Dogs actually have different tones in their growls. A higher pitched growl, for example, usually means that the dog wants to be left alone. Lower growls may mean an attack is imminent. He may be afraid or in pain. He may be protecting his toys, turf, or bed. He may be growling when cornering a mouse or rabbit. Dogs also growl in play, such as when playing tug-of-war.

Solution

In general, it is best to respect a growling dog. Don't try to "show the dog who's boss." This is the kind of behavior that leads to being bitten. If your Beagle growls at you when you try to remove him from the chair, offer him some cheese to get him off. Then, don't let the dog back on the chair. Establish a firm leadership and your dog will soon not think of challenging it. If he does, consult a behaviorist or your vet. Again, however, this nasty sort of behavior is extremely rare in Beagles. It's one of the reasons why Beagles are just about the best dogs in the world.

A well-trained Beagle is a joy to be around. In fact, training will build his self-confidence, which in turn will help your dog become a valued companion and member of the family.

ADVANCED TRAINING AND ACTIVITIES
F O R   Y O U R   B E A G L E

Once your Beagle is reasonably well trained, socialized, and adjusted to your lifestyle, it's time to think about broadening his horizons. There are many canine activities for him (and you) to enjoy. Try several of the ones listed here, and see which ones appeal to you both.

Before engaging in any performance activity, though, have your dog checked out by the vet to be sure he's in good shape, and begin slowly!

THE CANINE GOOD CITIZEN® PROGRAM

The American Kennel Club's Canine Good Citizen (CGC) Program is a certification program that is designed to reward dogs who have good manners at home and in the community. The two parts of the program stress responsible pet ownership for owners and basic good manners for dogs. All dogs who pass the ten-step test may receive an official, frame-worthy certificate from the American Kennel Club.

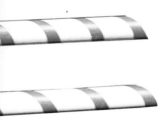

The Canine Good Citizen test is open to all dogs, whether mixed breed or purebred, and there is no age limit, although the dog must be old enough to have received his immunizations. You will need a leash and collar (buckle or slip-type collar; no special training collars, such as a prong collar or head halter, are permitted) and a brush or comb for grooming. Your dog should be well groomed and in healthy condition.

This is a great opportunity to educate, bond, and have fun with your dog. You'll both benefit!

CONFORMATION (DOG SHOWS)

Conformation showing is a beauty contest. (It's what you see at the Westminster Dog Show every February on television.) For most people, the goal of conformation showing is to win a Championship. To do this, a dog needs to accumulate 15 points at AKC-sanctioned dog shows. Dogs can win as many as five points at a given show, although this is very rare. More commonly, a dog will win one, two, or three points. The number of points your dog can win depends on how many other Beagles were entered in all of the classes.

A dog show is an event at which dogs compete to see which of them most closely resembles the breed standard. They are judged both standing and trotting ("gaiting") around the ring. They move in straight lines, circles, and triangles, with you at the end of the lead. When standing, you may decide to "stack" your dog, or you may decide to "free bait" him. In a stack, the dog is held by the handler, with one hand on the neck and the other on the tail (usually holding it up). In a free bait, the handler stands away from the dog and the dog stands at attention. This is more natural and beautiful, but not enough people work at getting that

In a stack, the dog is held by the handler, with one hand on the neck and the other on the tail.

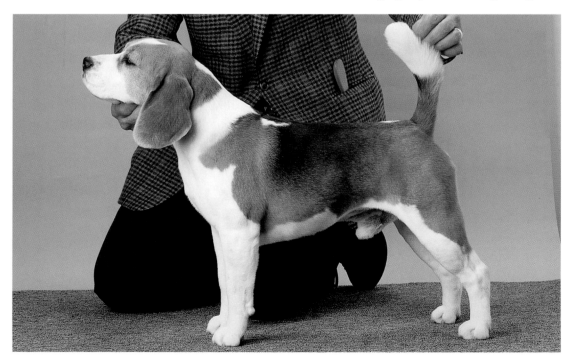

A good handler has the ability to show your Beagle to his best advantage.

wonderful response! If you are interested in this sport, get a mentor, preferably someone from your local Beagle club or kennel club to help you out.

Next to the Kentucky Derby, the Westminster Dog Show is the oldest, most continuous sporting event held in the United States. The original "Westminster" was actually a bar in a hotel of the same name. (The hotel no longer exists.) The first members of the Westminster Kennel Club were men who owned gundogs, and even today the logo of the show is a representation of Sensation, a pointer owned by one of the members who had a legendary ability to point birds. In 1877, the club held its first dog show, called the "First Annual New York Bench Show of Dogs." Since 1883, the Westminster Dog Show has been held in Madison Square Garden in New York. So far, a Beagle has not attained the title Best in Show, but there's always next year!

Crufts Versus Westminster

Crufts is Britain's answer to Westminster, but it's a very different show. And although both shows are run under the auspices of their respective national clubs—the AKC in the United States and the Kennel Club in the UK—the two events are very different. Crufts is much more casual and relaxed, and it is more of a family affair. It features not just conformation but also agility, flyball, dancing, and duck herding. Crufts is named for its founder, Charles Cruft, a "dog cake" salesman who organized the first show in 1891. The show was very successful and continued to run after Cruft died in 1938. His widow ran the show in 1939. The show was interrupted by World War II and its chaotic aftermath but returned under the auspices of the Kennel Club in 1948.

The Kennel Club recognizes 197 different breeds and divides them into the following categories:

- Hounds
- Gundogs
- Terriers
- Utility
- Working
- Pastoral
- Toy

There are restrictions that keep certain top Crufts dogs from competing at Westminster, and vice versa. Ear cropping, for example, is part of the breed standard for some breeds in the United States, but this practice is forbidden in many European countries, including the UK. Fortunately, the Beagle is shown *au naturel* in the United States, meaning no cropped ears or docked tails for this spunky little guy!

OBEDIENCE

Formal obedience competition is an honored tradition in the world of purebred dogs. And while the independent Beagle will never be real competition for a Golden Retriever, your Beagle can still participate in and even win an obedience title if you have the patience to work with him.

Like a good conformation dog, an obedience dog needs to have good structure, good movement, and an attentive personality. Shy, oversubmissive, or dominant dogs have temperament problems that make them less suitable for this demanding sport.

Obedience training is the bedrock of all canine sports and companion activities. A willful, disobedient dog cannot achieve success in tracking, conformation, agility, search and rescue, or any of the other myriad activities human do with their dogs unless they are proficient at obedience.

When begun in 1933, AKC obedience trials were designed to foster training and demonstrate a dog's willingness to work closely with people. Today, obedience

The reason that hounds in general do not excel in obedience is that they were bred to take the lead—they run after a rabbit, and you follow them. Retrievers were bred to work more closely with their human partner and are thus more naturally obedient.

trials are held at most all-breed dog shows. Obedience trials were originally created to have several levels, including the long-standing classes of Novice (CD), Open (CDX), and Utility (UD). Later, higher levels of competition were added, like Utility Excellent (UDX) and Obedience Trial Champion (OTCH). The newest title will be awarded to the top dog at the National Obedience Invitational. This dog will become the National Obedience Champion for the entire year.

To receive a "leg" toward his obedience title, all your dog needs to do is to pass the required events for his level. Currently, there are three levels of Obedience: Novice, Open, and Utility. The Novice and Open levels are further divided into two classes, A and B, with the A classes created for people who have not competed successfully at that level yet, and the B classes for more experienced handlers. Every competition is worth 200 points, and to qualify, your Beagle must earn 170 of those points. He has to do this three times under three different judges. If he does, he wins his CD (Companion Dog) title. Higher level competition results in CDX (Companion Dog Excellent) and UD (Utility Dog) titles. Dogs who have earned their UD are eligible to win the coveted OTCH (Obedience Trial Champion), a title earned by outscoring other dogs at several events.

To attain the first of these degrees, the CD, a dog must heel on leash, heel free, stand for examination, recall, and complete a long sit (one minute) and a long down (three minutes). When heeling, he'll have to execute left and right turns, stops, and move at various speeds. On the "stand," he'll need to stand still off lead while a judge examines him. The handler must be at least 6 feet away. The recall requires the dog to sit 30 feet from the handler, come quickly, and then sit. On command, the dog will move to the heel position and sit once more.

Earning a CDX title requires your dog to work entirely off lead. He will have to heel off lead in a figure 8 pattern, drop on recall (going "down" rather than just sitting), retrieve a dumbbell from 20 feet over level ground, retrieve a dumbbell over the high jump, and jump the broad jump. He must also do longer sits (three minutes) and downs (five minutes) with the handler completely out of sight.

Utility dogs must follow hand signals for heeling, moving, and standing for examination. The handler cannot

Freestyle Obedience
Freestyle obedience emphasizes not only classic obedience skills, but also bows, weaves, backups, and jumps, all choreographed to music like a dance. Freestyle obedience focuses on creativity and the synchronicity between the dog and human partner. Visit the Canine Freestyle Federation at www.canine-freestyle.org for more information.

use voice signals in this section. Dogs also participate in directed jumping, directed retrieve, and scent discrimination. Dogs can work for their Utility and CDX degrees at the same time.

A new AKC obedience sport is rally obedience, and Beagles seem to be more suited for this than regular obedience. In rally obedience, the owner is allowed to talk to and encourage the dog. In addition, the dog moves though a course that Beagles seem to enjoy very much.

AGILITY

Beagles are agile little fellas, and if yours will obey simple commands, he's a natural for this sport! Agility has become extremely popular among dog owners, and it has three levels: Novice, Open, and Excellent. Two types are offered at each level: standard or jumpers with weave poles. For example, at the Novice "standard" level, a dog dashes through an obstacle course consisting of ramps, seesaws, "dog-walks," tunnels, jumps, and a "pause table." The weave pole level adds the weave poles and omits the pause table, along with some other minor differences.

It's important to remember that agility places stress and compressive force on young, developing joints. Many agility experts recommend waiting until your dog is 18 to 24 months old, when his skeletal system is more mature. Begin with lower jumps and slower speeds for your young Beagle,

Agility competition is a great way to exercise your Beagle's natural intelligence.

building up only gradually. You should also check your dog daily for lameness or swelling.

In the United States, several organizations hold sanctioned agility events. These include the AKC, the United States Dog Agility Association, and the North American Dog Agility Council, Inc. (NADAC).

FLYBALL

Flyball is a team sport for dogs that was invented in California during the 1970s. It is a relay race that features four dogs per team. The course has four hurdles spaced 10 feet apart and a spring-loaded box that shoots out a tennis ball. The hurdles' height is dependent on the height of the dogs in the team—4 inches below the shoulder height of the shortest dog. Eight inches is the minimum height, and 16 inches is the maximum height. Each dog jumps the hurdles and presses the box to catch the ball and then runs back over the four hurdles. When the dog crosses the starting line, the next dog goes. The first team to have all four dogs run without errors wins the heat. Beagles can be naturals at flyball because they are fast and agile, as long as you can get them to bring back the ball!

TRACKING

AKC tracking is a wonderful sport open to all breeds. In tracking, the dog follows a human scent (embedded in an article like a leather glove) around a very large outdoor

Due to their wonderful noses, Beagles are potentially great tracking dogs.

Advanced Training and Activities for Your Beagle 123

course. The problem is that while Beagles have wonderful noses, they can be easily distracted by the scent of rabbits that may cross the trail. It takes a lot of discipline for the Beagle to ignore his heritage and ignore the rabbit while following a boring human scent. Beagles have the ability to be great tracking dogs—it's the willingness to do it that makes for the challenge.

FIELD TRIALS AND BEAGLING

If the outdoors is your style, you have a choice of several Beagle activities to enjoy. You can, of course, merely trot off into the woods and go rabbit hunting with your hound. However, there are more formal activities available as well.

Field Trials

One of the best known outdoor activities are field trials. The AKC has licensed Beagle field trials for more than 105 years! There is no required dress code for this activity, and participants usually wear comfortable clothing.

Field trial Beagles were developed from cottontail hunting Beagles. The AKC requires that every field trial Beagle Club have its own fenced grounds for field trialing. Today, more than 529 Beagle clubs own or lease land in excess of 150 acres each. It is believed that the fencing actually makes the rabbits even more likely to attempt to hide and go to ground. Indeed, rabbits living in field trial areas behave quite differently from their wild cousins. Field trial Beagles have extremely keen noses and move slowly (*very* slowly) and meticulously over the land in search of their quarry. You may be happy to know that the rabbits are not killed, only found.

Drag Meets

A drag hunt or drag meeting is an event common in European countries, usually occurring from October to March. In this event, a pack of hounds (traditionally foxhounds, but Beagles participate, too) follows a line of artificial scent made up of various substances, mostly animal droppings fixed in paraffin with aniseed added to strengthen the scent. The substances are then laid out in sections across the countryside by a person on horseback known as the dragsperson. The substances are sometimes crammed in a rabbit skin and pulled along through the grass. The objective, of course, is to see how well the hounds can follow the scent, which holds for about 45 minutes. The great thing about drag hunting is that no animals are killed or even chased. Hounds who are considered by the judges to be "doing the job" are given a Working Certificate.

Field trial Beagles are run in a brace (group of two or three). The winners are the dogs who show the most "style." Some rabbit hunters became quite disturbed at the trend toward slow-motion Beagles and pressed for a new way of working Beagles: the Small Pack Option (SPO). These dogs are tested in somewhat more real hunting conditions and are also tested for gun shyness. They are first trained in 10-acre, 40-acre, and 100-acre enclosures to learn the ropes. Then, they are put with young, aggressive Beagles to see how they work together. Small Pack Option divides the dogs into packs of seven to pursue rabbits. There now also exists a Large Pack trial in which all of the dogs in the class are turned loose to find and track hares. Most Large Pack dogs begin with rabbits, however. A pack of 30 to 60 hounds or more in a single class is not uncommon. These dogs really move, sometimes so fast a person on a horse can't keep up.

Beagles who do a lot of hunting and field work are especially in need of a high protein diet to maintain their blood sugar level. Certain families of Beagles are prone to so-called "running fits" (seizures that occur if glucose levels get too low) that seem connected with a drop in glucose.

Beagling
Today, thousands of people all around the world hunt with Beagles, either individually or in Beagle packs

throughout the country. Packs are hunted in the ancient manner using a regular hunt staff wearing hunt liveries with their own distinctive colors. This sport is extremely popular in the United Kingdom and has its aficionados in the United States as well. It is not the same thing as field trials, and the dogs look quite different from show Beagles. In this sport, the rabbit is usually killed. Often there are 25 to 30 hound couples in the kennels, and hunts take place twice a week. (A "couple" is simply two dogs, as the name suggests. Hounds are always counted in couples.) Packs are often made up of all males or all females, although they can be mixed.

Hunting Beagles are started when they are around six to nine months of age. Most young Beagles start running by sight-chasing a rabbit a few times until they lose sight of him. Eventually, a Beagle figures out that using his nose will help him keep track of the rabbit even after it disappears. Most hunters start them out alone before putting them with other Beagles. (The dog will be more desperate to keep up with the others than following the rabbit.) If you're short of rabbits, you can hire someone to "start" the Beagle for you.

Some Beagles are trained to hunt cottontail rabbits, while others are trained to hunt hares. Rabbits are smaller, with a weaker scent; they run in small swings and tend to go to ground. The hare has a stronger smell, wider swing, and does not go to ground. Remember that field trial dogs, show dogs, and hunting dogs are all bred from different lines, because the handlers are looking for different things from each. And even though it may seem that field trialing is very much the same as hunting, in field trials (especially brace) the judges are looking for dogs who scent track more slowly and carefully than real life hunters want.

SERVICE AND THERAPY DOGS

There are about 15,000 service dogs working in the United States. They provide assistance to the disabled, comfort to the elderly, and guidance to the blind. While you can't expect your merry little Beagle to be a guide dog (he is too small and independent), he is a truly perfect dog for therapy.

Since 1990, the Delta Society has offered its Pet Partners Program, a program that screens and trains human and canine volunteers to visit people in hospitals, prisons, schools, and nursing homes. There are currently more than 5,400 human-dog teams helping almost a million people in the United States and six other countries around the world.

EXERCISE, GAMES, AND ACTIVITIES

Maybe you're not interested in organized events. That's fine, because you and your Beagle can have a great time just by yourselves!

Walking and Jogging

Walking or jogging is a great way to bond with your dog in a healthful, low-stress event that you'll both like. It has been shown that people who have a dog buddy for a walking partner do better than those people who do it alone—and your dog will enjoy it as well!

If you decide to walk or jog with your Beagle, begin slowly. Work up to a half hour or so of vigorous activity several times a week.

This is a great way to get needed exercise and stimulate your Beagle's mind and senses at

Making sure your Beagle gets plenty of exercise is key to maintaining his good health.

the same time. Speaking of senses, your dog is bound to get thirsty as you go. You may have a canteen or sports bottle, but what does your Beagle have? Certainly you don't expect him to drink water out of dirty ponds or even deceptively clear-looking streams. These natural sources of water can be loaded with toxins, bacteria, and parasites. Some people bring along extra water and dishes for their dogs, but if you forgot, you can actually teach your Beagle to drink out of your own sport squirt bottle. To train him, start at home, when he's thirsty. Squirt the water into his normal water bowl. He may be nervous at first, but thirst will win out. Squirt the water in very slowly, more slowly than the dog will actually drink it. After a few seconds, your Beagle will probably start licking the bottle itself rather than waiting for the bowl to fill. (Beagles are not known for their patience.) Turn the bottle to the side of his mouth and step up the pressure *slightly* so the water runs over his tongue. Don't hold the bottle too high, as a dog normally drinks with his muzzle pointed down. Don't just squirt it down his throat, either. He's not accustomed to it yet and might gag or choke. Soon, he'll figure out how to drink from your bottle without contaminating it, and you'll be on the road to a great hike with your pal!

Tug-of-War

For a long time, people were told not to play tug with their dogs, as it made them aggressive and dominant. This is not true, although you probably should avoid this game with an animal who has had domination or aggression problems in the past. For the normal Beagle, however, tug-of-war is a perfectly suitable game. It provides great exercise and can be played in a small area.

Select a simple tug toy like a tug rope that the dog will come to recognize as the cue for the game, and use it only for tug-of-war. Devise a special command to begin the game, like "let's tug!" Your dog will naturally want to grab the tug rope. If he grabs the rope without permission, don't play—he should release it on command. If he does not do this, teach him by trading the rope for a treat. As soon as you get the rope from him, give it right back and praise him. This will make him more amenable to giving up his cherished rope. If he runs off with the toy, don't chase him. He'll soon return with it for more tugs.

You can also interrupt the game with a few obedience commands from time to time. This will sharpen his skills and keep him listening to you. Don't allow the dog to touch you with his teeth. If you receive a nip, stop the game immediately for at least five minutes. He'll get the picture.

Fetch

Although teaching a Beagle to fetch may seem like a waste of time, it's an indispensable skill for guide, bomb detection, and search and rescue dogs.

Most Beagles will chase after a ball, but when they get it they not only won't bring it back, they will run away with it. To get your Beagle to bring the ball back, you may have to turn and run in the opposite direction so that he's chasing you. When he comes up, take the toy and reward him. Try again. If your Beagle shows no interest in chasing the ball, your job becomes harder. You may have to rub some peanut butter on it. Or, you may think, "Hmm, how important is it really that my Beagle fetches? Is it not enough that he comes, sits, heels, and is the sweetest dog in the world?"

Hunting

I'm not a hunter myself, but if you enjoy this sport, you certainly can't go wrong with a Beagle as your hunting pal. If you are training your Beagle to hunt, most authorities recommend you start with a four-month-old puppy. That way you won't have to train your adult dog out of the many bad habits he has probably acquired over the years.

The first step is to introduce the dog to the scent of a wild rabbit. Some trainers kill a rabbit and tie it to a drag cord (an old washcloth and 4-foot cord); others use rabbit scent you can buy in hunting supply stores. Saturate the washcloth with the scent of the rabbit, and drag a trail. Then, put your puppy on the ground at the start of the trail. It won't be long before he picks up the scent. With each session, make the trail a little longer. Damp earth and overcast weather are best for tracking scents.

When he's five months old, he's ready for his first walk in the woods! It's odd, but in Beagle work, you need to encourage the dog to go in front of you, not trailing behind or at heel. That's one thing that makes it confusing for puppies to figure out. Some trainers use different collars on the dog for different events, and the dog learns what's expected of him that day by the collar he is wearing.

Remember that you will have to desensitize your hunting dog to gunfire. Dogs don't naturally take to loud noises, so this is something you'll have to work at. You can begin by introducing loud sounds while he is eating. Eating is so important to most Beagles that it makes up for almost anything!

Of course, if you plan to hunt with your Beagle, you need to learn the rules, obtain the proper licenses, and learn gun safety. One of the best ways to do this is to get a mentor.

As you can see, there are numerous joys to owning a Beagle. These independent but fun-loving dogs have the potential to excel at a variety of endeavors!

Hare hunting Beagles are bigger, longer legged, and have greater endurance than rabbit hunting or field trial dogs. The dogs run for two hours, and then there's a judge's conference to eliminate the less successful hounds. The judges meet periodically, eliminating more dogs at each conference. However, the "eliminated" hounds continue to run with the brace. They don't know they're out of the game.

HEALTH

OF YOUR BEAGLE

Your Beagle's health is more important than almost anything else, and it's up to you to maintain it. You'll need all of your owner savvy to keep a careful eye on your dog. In fact, you are his first line of defense against illness, and your vet is your backup and support. In many cases, you can prevent your Beagle from getting sick in the first place by making sure he gets a proper diet, the right amount of exercise, and appropriate preventive care, like vaccinations and antiparasite medications.

PHYSICAL EXAMINATIONS

Having regular checkups is probably even more important for dogs than for people, and the reason is simple. A dog cannot explain to his owner when he feels sick, and so he depends upon his owners to examine him regularly. The best start to all of this is a routine physical so that any problems can be spotted early and fixed before they turn into something serious.

The First Visit

Make the first visit to the vet a fun and interesting one for your dog. If all goes well, the first trip will be for a checkup only, so your dog won't have any painful associations with the visit. If you are calm and happy yourself, your mood is bound to rub off on your Beagle! It's really important to use this first visit as an opportunity to establish a cordial relationship between your vet and your dog. Your dog will have no reason to fear the vet if you don't.

Do not wait until your puppy is sick before he meets his doctor for the first time. A healthy, bouncy puppy will have no fear of the vet unless it's instilled in him by your own insecurities. Make the trip fun by giving him treats and keeping your tone of voice excited and happy when speaking to him.

During that all-important first visit, your vet will weigh your puppy and take his temperature and pulse. She will listen to the heart and lungs through a stethoscope and palpate the organs to feel for any abnormalities. Your vet will also check your dog's genitals to make sure there is no unusual discharge, and in the case of unneutered males, she will ensure that the testicles are properly descending. In addition, she will examine your dog's eyes and ears and check the skin for parasites and general tone. The dental check is critical, too. Baby teeth sometimes don't fall

A routine physical is a good way to detect any potential medical problems early.

out when they should, and older dogs may need their teeth cleaned.

Routine Checkups

The routine physical exam actually begins before the vet even touches your dog. It starts with you providing important information on a questionnaire or through a discussion with your vet about your Beagle's health history and current behavior. Everything you can tell the vet is helpful to ensuring your dog's wellness.

The actual physical part of the examination usually begins with a check of the nose and mouth. The vet will perform a dental check and then examine the face and head to check the neurological function of the cranial nerves.

Neutering (Spaying and Castrating)

Unless you own a show dog, please consider spaying or castrating your Beagle. Spaying a female dog refers to the removal of the ovaries and uterus, while castration refers to the removal of a male dog's testicles. Neutering has numerous health benefits, such as eliminating or reducing the risk of various cancers of the reproductive system, including prostate cancer in males and mammary cancer in females. It also eliminates the possibility of uterine infections in females. Additionally, neutering your pet will help ease the problem of dog overpopulation. Right now, there are not enough good homes for all of the dogs who are born every day. Even if you could find homes for all of your dog's puppies, what about their puppies? At one time, it was believed that dogs could not be safely neutered before the age of six months; however, modern advances in surgery have made early neutering and spaying possible.

Use your first visit to the vet as an opportunity to establish a good relationship between your vet and your dog.

She'll lift the ear flap and give those generous Beagle ears a good inspection for infection or mites. She will also part the fur and check the skin for fleas and signs of allergy and infection. The vet will then palpate the neck to check for abnormalities in the lymph nodes or thyroid area. Other lymph nodes in shoulder and armpit areas will warrant a careful inspection as well. In addition, she will palpate the dog's muscles and extend and bend your Beagle's legs to test for reflexes or pain. She'll listen to your dog's heart and lungs through a stethoscope and then check for abnormalities of the kidneys, liver, and intestines. (Many times abnormalities can be felt right through the skin by an experienced examiner as lumps or by a painful reaction from the dog.) A rectal exam will also be performed, and the vet will take his temperature. If appropriate, your vet may also administer vaccinations.

In some cases, a fecal exam, urinalysis, complete blood cell count, or complete chemistry panel may be performed. If an illness is suspected, specific blood tests or x-rays may be ordered. The vet may also recommend you see a specialist if she feels there's a potential problem out of her field of expertise. (More than 20 areas of veterinary specialty are recognized by the American Veterinary Medical Association, and veterinary specialty clinics are becoming more common.)

VACCINATIONS

Vaccinations save lives. Before the days of effective

Veterinary Specializations

Veterinary medicine has grown so much in the past quarter century that vets, like physicians, often specialize. Specializations include critical care, internal medicine, oncology (cancer treatment), cardiology, surgery, dentistry, dermatology, ophthalmology (eye care), anesthesia, theriogenology (reproductive medicine), and radiology. Getting "board-certified" in an area usually requires a one-year internship (or an equivalent in experience which can count as an internship) and a residency. Most residency programs last three years. After the residency, the practitioner must pass an approved board examination to become a diplomate of a particular specialty college (an association of specialists that regulate credentials in their area).

veterinary vaccines, dogs were victims of canine distemper, hepatitis, and rabies. Now these diseases are rare. When parvovirus first emerged on the scene in the late 1970s, many dogs died before a vaccine was developed. While there is an ongoing discussion about how often and against what diseases your dog needs to be vaccinated, you owe it to your dog and your community to do your research and make an informed choice. Of course, as with any medical procedure, adverse reactions or side effects can occur. Usually these are minor, especially when compared to the risks of developing the disease Consult with your veterinarian to inquire about her vaccine protocol, and don't be afraid to ask questions!

How Vaccines Work

A vaccine works by priming an animal's immune response against a specific disease. The vaccine stimulates the immune system with a nonpathogenic virus or bacteria, one that has been killed or modified in such a way that it no longer poses a danger to the pet. The dog then develops "memory cells" that help fight off the dangerous pathogenic form of the virus when it is later encountered.

In order to obtain the best response from a vaccine, puppies and unvaccinated older dogs are given repeated doses. Puppies receive multiple vaccines every two to four weeks to stimulate the immune system to achieve a long-term response at the time that the mother's antibodies disappear. As long as the maternal antibodies are present, the pup will have some protection against diseases, but he will not receive long-term protection from a vaccination.

Check with your veterinarian to determine the right vaccination schedule for your Beagle.

Although it is commonly believed that a certain number of vaccinations must be given, the number of injections has nothing to do with immunity. Protection is achieved by giving a vaccine at a time when maternal antibodies won't interfere. (This doesn't apply to rabies vaccines, however. Rabies vaccines are in a somewhat different category, as they are given with killed, rather than a modified live vaccine.)

Newborn puppies cannot be vaccinated because they have inherited some protection in the form of antibodies from their mothers that will block the commercial vaccine. Only when the maternal antibodies drop will a commercial vaccine become effective. Unfortunately, there is a dangerous window when the maternal antibodies are too low to protect the puppy but still high enough to block the commercial vaccine. At this time, the puppy is most at risk for many viral diseases. The length and timing of this window is variable from litter to litter and even from puppy to puppy.

Vaccination Protocol

In general, six to nine weeks is the earliest and safest time to inaugurate a commercial vaccination program, although some veterinarians recommend administering a parvovirus vaccine at five weeks of age. Vaccinating puppies any younger than this, especially with modified live vaccines, can lead to problems. Remember, vaccines do not work immediately; a minimum of five days must pass before you can say that your dog is safely vaccinated.

Puppy Vaccination Schedule

Age	Vaccination
5 weeks	**Parvovirus:** For puppies at high risk of exposure to parvo, some veterinarians recommend vaccinating at 5 weeks.
6-9 weeks	Combination vaccine without leptospirosis. **Coronavirus:** Where coronavirus is prevalent.
12 weeks or older	**Rabies:** Given by your local veterinarian (age at vaccination may vary according to local law).
12-15 weeks	Combination vaccine **Leptospirosis:** Include leptospirosis in the combination vaccine where leptospirosis is a concern, or if traveling to an area where it occurs. **Coronavirus:** Where coronavirus is a concern. **Lyme:** Where Lyme disease is prevalent or if you're going somewhere it is prevalent.
Adult (boosters)	Combination vaccine **Leptospirosis:** Include leptospirosis in the combo vaccine where leptospirosis is a problem if you're going somewhere it is prevalent. **Coronavirus:** Where coronavirus is a concern. **Lyme:** Where Lyme disease is a problem or if you're going somewhere it is prevalent. **Rabies:** Given by your local veterinarian (stipulated interval between vaccinations varies according to state or local law, usually one to three years). Most vets now give booster shots only every three years. Annual vaccinations are no longer considered necessary.

The AVMA Council on Biologic and Therapeutic Agents' Report on Cat and Dog Vaccines has recommended that the core (essential) vaccines for dogs include distemper, canine adenovirus-2 (hepatitis and respiratory disease), and canine parvovirus-2.

Noncore vaccines include leptospirosis, coronavirus, canine parainfluenza and *Bordetella bronchiseptica* (both factors in kennel cough), and *Borrelia burgdorferi* (Lyme disease). Talk to your vet about what is necessary in your area.

The following is a possible vaccination schedule for the average puppy. However, your dog is an individual, so it's important to check with your vet to see what is best for him.

Diseases to Protect Against

Although vaccination protocols differ from place to place and even from vet to vet, you should vaccinate your Beagle puppy against the diseases described below.

Rabies

This fatal disease is caused by a virus and is transmitted through contact with the saliva of an infected animal, usually through a bite. After multiplying within these bite wound tissues, the virus migrates to the central nervous system, where it causes widespread destruction of nerve tissue and inflammation in the brain and spinal cord. Any mammal can contract rabies, although raccoons, skunks, foxes, bats, and occasionally groundhogs are the most common victims.

The incubation period can last from several weeks to a year or more. Once an animal is infected, the virus travels along the nerves to the spinal cord and then to the brain. To make things worse, you can never be absolutely certain that a dog has contracted rabies just by observation, because the signs are extremely variable and often mimic those of other disease. Some dogs become aggressive, while others become confused and disoriented. There is no known cure for the disease, and if not treated immediately, it is fatal.

Parvovirus

Since 1978, dogs of all ages and breeds have been victims of a highly contagious viral disease called parvovirus (parvo). Parvovirus strikes the intestinal tract, white blood cells, and in some cases, the heart muscle. The disease is characterized by smelly diarrhea that is often bloody, vomiting, dehydration, and in severe cases, fever and lowered white blood cell count. The virus attacks the lining of the small intestine of all canines, not just dogs. Death can occur as early as two days after the onset of the disease. Vaccinations have helped to control the spread of parvovirus, but despite being vaccinated, some dogs still contract the disease and often die from it. Puppies under 12 weeks old are most severely affected, but many infected adults demonstrate few, if any, signs.

Not all cases of bloody diarrhea and vomiting result from parvo. The only sure way to know is through a diagnostic test your vet can give.

The normal incubation period for parvo is 7 to 14 days. The virus is shed in the feces beginning the third day after exposure, often before clinical signs appear, and may last for one to two weeks after the onset of the disease. This villainous virus is a very stable pathogen that survives on inanimate objects, including clothing, food pans, and cage floors for five months or even longer under the right conditions. Insects and rodents may also play an important role in the transmission of the disease.

Exposure to ultraviolet light and a bleach solution of 1/2 cup of bleach to 1 gallon of water can inactivate parvovirus. Treatment for the disease is mostly supportive and includes replacing fluids lost through vomiting and diarrhea, usually by intravenous administration of a balanced electrolyte solution. Antibiotics are given to help control secondary bacterial infections. If severe vomiting is present, drugs may also be used to slow the vomiting. Still, even with the best available care, the mortality of severely infected animals is high. The parvovirus vaccine should be administered to your Beagle every 3 to 4 weeks from 6 to 16 weeks of age.

Coronavirus

Like parvo, coronavirus attacks the small intestinal lining. Signs of the disease include lethargy, anorexia, depression, sudden vomiting, and diarrhea with yellow-orange stools. The diarrhea may be bloody. Where coronavirus is a problem, vaccination is usually given at 12 weeks with a booster at 16 weeks, but older dogs aren't usually vaccinated.

As with parvovirus, treatment for coronavirus is mostly supportive and includes replacing fluids lost through vomiting and diarrhea.

Distemper

Canine distemper is a highly infectious disease actually related to human measles. About 85 percent of dogs who develop clinical signs of the disease will die. Younger dogs and puppies are the most susceptible to infection. Distemper is spread through the air and is most severe when it attacks puppies under the age of three months. Early clinical signs include anorexia, diarrhea, and dehydration. As the disease progresses, fever, coughing, inflammation of the tissues around the nose and eyes, depression, vomiting, and bloody diarrhea will develop. Even dogs who recover may have lifelong complications, especially of the nervous system. Total paralysis may even result. Supportive treatment like IV fluids is all that can usually be given to treat distemper. The distemper vaccine should be administered every 3 to 4 weeks from 6 to 16 weeks of age.

Leptospirosis

Leptospirosis is a bacterial infectious disease characterized by depression, congested mucous membranes, fever, and loss of appetite. The pathogen is shed in the urine of affected animals. It can affect both the kidneys and liver. Signs include vomiting, dehydration, excessive urination, and excessive thirst. Treatment includes antibiotics and in cases of kidney failure, dialysis. Many commercially available distemper/parvovirus vaccines also include lepto in their combinations.

Bordetellosis (Kennel Cough)

Kennel cough is a common disease that can be caused by a variety of organisms. The virus is airborne, and to make things worse, it can be carried along in moisture, mold, or dust for very long distances. Your dog can also get the disease from a carrier dog who appears to be healthy.

The primary sign of kennel cough is a frequent, hacking, harsh cough that may last for two to three weeks. Usually the infection is mild and self-limiting, lasting five to ten days. Some dogs do well with a cough suppressant, while others need antibiotics, especially if a fever is present or if there are complications such as bacterial pneumonia. Older dogs are at greatest risk of the disease. Your vet can vaccinate your dog against this disease through the use of a nasal spray or an injectable immunization.

Adverse Reactions

In rare cases, your dog might react negatively to a vaccine. Reactions vary with the type of vaccine used and the age of the vaccinated animal. However, compared to the dangers of not vaccinating, the risks are tiny. The most severe and rarest (1 in every 15,000 vaccinations) reaction is anaphylaxis, a life-threatening, immediate allergic reaction to something injected. Anaphylactic reactions are more commonly associated with the use of killed vaccines like rabies, canine coronavirus, and leptospirosis. That's because killed vaccines have more viral or bacterial particles per dose and also have added chemicals to boost the dog's immune response. These same features increase the risk of an allergic response.

If untreated, anaphylaxis results in shock, respiratory distress, and cardiac failure. This reaction usually occurs within minutes to less than 24 hours of the vaccination. If you think your dog is having an anaphylactic reaction, get him emergency veterinary care right away. Epinephrine should be given as soon as possible. Your vet may also want to administer intravenous fluids, oxygen, and other medications.

Kennel cough can spread very rapidly through a kennel, causing dogs to cough, wheeze, hack, and sneeze.

PARASITES

Parasites make their living off your dog, and most of them make your dog sick in the process. However, there's no need for this! Nearly all diseases resulting from parasite infestation are completely preventable.

Parasites cause problems that can result in something as simple as mild itching or something much more severe, such as death. External parasites include mites (sarcoptic, demodex, ear, and cheyletiella), fleas, and ticks. Internal parasites usually include worms like roundworm, hookworm, whipworm, tapeworm, and heartworm. Many of these parasites can be prevented or kept under control with preventive medications.

External Parasites

External parasites live on but not inside your dog's body. With the exception of some species of mites, they are usually visible.

Fleas

More than 2,200 species of fleas exist worldwide, but fortunately, most of them live elsewhere than on your Beagle. In fact, there is no reason for the contemporary dog to become afflicted with fleas. It still happens, though, and the ingestion of even one flea containing a tapeworm larva is enough to transmit tapeworm. It can even cause an allergic dog to develop itchy flea dermatitis, which is caused by certain enzymes in flea saliva.

One of the most important things to remember when dealing with fleas is this: Don't wait for your pet to start scratching! Even if you use a good flea preventive, it doesn't hurt to check your dog for fleas every time you groom him. Glide your thumbs against the growth pattern of the fur, or use a flea comb. The groin, base of the tail, and neck are popular flea hangouts. Even if you don't see any actual fleas, the black deposits they leave will provide a clue to their presence.

In the old days, people tried to control fleas with topical sprays, powders, dips, collars, and yard sprays. While some people still resort to these old-fashioned methods, most up-to-date owners choose to control fleas with a capsule, or they use a spot-on liquid applied to the skin between the shoulder blades. Some products are available from your veterinarian, although you can get others (even though they are somewhat shorter lived and less effective) at the pet supply or grocery store. Some people have also had luck with natural alternatives to conventional flea or tick medications. Not all natural alternatives are equally effective, however. It's important to consult with your veterinarian before selecting a particular remedy.

Ticks

Ticks are actually members of the spider family (arthropods) that spread diseases that attack both people and dogs. These include Lyme disease, Rocky Mountain spotted fever, relapsing fever, and ehrlichiosis. In fact, ticks spread more diseases than any other arthropod, and there are more than 850 species of ticks that parasitize every class of land vertebrate known. Conventional tick season is April through September (ticks like high humidity and moderate temperatures), but the truth is that ticks can become activated at any time the temperature reaches 40°F.

Do not despair, though, because some of the same products used on fleas will work on ticks as well. A residual insecticide, for example, will kill all ticks. There are also special collars impregnated with amitraz (a parasite killer) specifically designed to target ticks, and these are great if your Beagle spends a lot of time outdoors. It's best to consult with your veterinarian to determine what antitick product is best for your Beagle.

Currently, researchers are working on a tick vaccine for dogs, and one for cattle is currently available. In the meantime, though, keep your Beagle safe by inspecting him for ticks after every romp in the woods. If you find any, remove them by pulling them straight out with a pair of tweezers. (Forget hot matches, petroleum jelly, nail polish, or alcohol. They don't work.) Once you get the tick out, flush it down the toilet. Be sure to wear gloves, and wash your hands afterward.

Mites

These arachnids appear in various species, several of which are troublesome to dogs.
• *Demodex canis* (demodectic mange or mange mites): Mange mites are nearly always

Check your dog for external parasites like fleas and ticks after he has been playing outdoors.

present somewhere on a dog (you have them, too—in your eyelashes and on your eyebrows), but they don't usually cause trouble, since the immune system keeps them well under control. Sometimes, however, the immune system doesn't do its job well. In that case, the mites multiply and crowd the hair follicles, causing them to fall out. The result is hair loss and itchy, swollen, red skin.

A localized form of mange may appear on puppies, who have immature immune systems, but it will probably resolve itself without treatment. A more serious, generalized form usually shows up on older dogs who also have a compromised immune system. This form requires intensive therapy involving dips in mite and tick killer. A complete cure may take up to six months. Generalized demodex is often a sign that the dog has another problem, like an autoimmune condition or a serious underlying disease, like cancer.

- *Sarcoptes scabiei* (**sarcoptic mange**): Sarcoptic mange is caused by the scabies mite, also known as the "itch mite." Both humans and dogs can get sarcoptic mange. People can contract a temporary case from their pets that lasts about six days, although these mites do not actually reproduce on humans. Puppies and young children are more likely to be affected than adults of either species. In dogs who are affected by the scabies mite, the female

If you treat your yard for fleas, allow the product to dry and bind to the grass before permitting Beagles and people into that yard.

burrows into the skin and lays her eggs. When they hatch into larvae, the larvae dig around and form nasty lesions, causing secondary infections. Affected dogs develop matted hair and a yellowish crust on their skin. This mange is treated with special shampoos, pills, or injections. A good insecticide needs to be applied to the entire area (including bedding) where the dog lives to prevent reinfection.

- *Cheyletiella yasguri* (**walking dandruff**): This mite's charming name is indicative of its uncharming habit of producing crud and hair loss on your dog. Fortunately, it doesn't cause the severe itchiness of the other mites and doesn't cause any really serious health problems. Your vet can easily treat it with a special pesticide.
- *Otodectes cynotis* (**ear mites**): The ear mite infests both the external ear and the ear canal, nibbling away at the loose skin there. Dogs with ear mites shake their heads and dig at their ears. There will be a nasty discharge or even a hematoma or swelling in the ear from self-mutilation.

To treat ear mites, the ear needs to be thoroughly cleaned and then treated with a good commercial ear mite killer. Over-the-counter treatments are available. However, because there are many causes of itchy ears that require different treatment protocols (and because home treatment can complicate the diagnosis for the vet), dogs with ear problems should be examined by a vet prior to treatment.

Internal Parasites

Parasites are so clever that they hide inside your dog where you can't see them. Just because you can't see them doesn't mean they can't do any harm, though. The danger with parasites is that they can do quite a lot of damage before you notice they are even present at all. This is an important reason to keep your dog on parasite preventive all year round.

Internal parasites can cause problems such as diarrhea, weight loss, anemia, dry hair, and vomiting. In some cases, there are no signs, and the worms can be passed from mothers to offspring during pregnancy. Common worms include the following:

Roundworm

Roundworms, the most common internal parasites, are found in the intestines of dogs. Practically all puppies are born with roundworms, because they are passed to puppies from their mothers before they are born, even if the mother is on an active worm preventative. Untreated, roundworms can infect vital organs, so puppies are usually "dewormed" when they are a few weeks old. Because puppies can begin passing roundworm eggs as early as three weeks, they should receive their first treatment for roundworm before this time.

Roundworms are spread when a dog ingests feces or soil contaminated with roundworm eggs. Older dogs tend not to become ill; the larvae remain dormant in the body. However, puppies can become very ill from them. Infected puppies have a distinct potbelly appearance, and they usually vomit and have a rough coat, bad breath, and diarrhea. Adult roundworms dwell in the intestine and live off ingested food.

One female roundworm can lay up to 200,000 eggs a day, which can only be destroyed through flame or steam. There are no chemicals that effectively kill the eggs. Unfortunately,

just a few eggs can lead to a large infestation. Since burning your house down isn't a good idea, kennels or other places where roundworm is a problem should be steam cleaned. The good news is that the eggs don't become "infective" for two to three weeks after they exit from the body (in feces). This is why picking up the yard is really important. You can throw the waste in the fire pit or place it in bags in the garbage. Flushing the waste down the toilet won't work because the eggs can survive sewage treatments.

Nearly all puppies are born with roundworms, because they are passed on from their mothers before they are born.

Hookworm

There are actually four species of hookworms that infect dogs (*Ancylostoma braziliense, Ancylostoma caninum, Ancylostoma tubaeforme,* and *Uncinaria stenocephala*). In dogs, *A. caninum* is the most common (and dangerous) hookworm. It can lead to severe anemia, especially in puppies.

Hookworms get their name from the hook-like "teeth" they use to attach to the intestinal wall. Hookworms are found mostly in warmer climates. They are very small (usually about 1/8 of an inch), but they can extract enormous amounts of blood from your dog, causing intestinal distress, bloody diarrhea, and in severe cases, anemia. Dogs can become infected with hookworm orally, through the skin, through the mother dog's placenta, and through the mother's milk. It has been reported that one adult female hookworm can produce as many as 20,000 eggs a day!

Your vet can detect hookworms easily though a microscopic examination of a stool sample. Adults can be

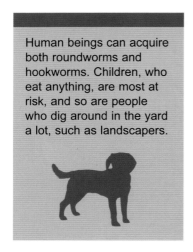

Human beings can acquire both roundworms and hookworms. Children, who eat anything, are most at risk, and so are people who dig around in the yard a lot, such as landscapers.

killed with several medications given orally or injected. Usually, the dog will require another treatment within two to four weeks. Most heartworm prevention products contain a drug that will prevent hookworm infections. However, these products will not kill adult hookworms, so dogs must be treated for adult hookworms first. The environment may also be treated, and some are even safe to use on grass.

Whipworm

Whipworm is one of the most common parasitic worms in North America, at least for dogs. It occurs much less frequently in cats and people. Adult whipworms live in the large intestine and ingest blood meals by attaching themselves to the intestinal lining, causing inflammation, anemia, blood diarrhea, and weight loss. The worms are then passed in the feces.

Diagnosis can be difficult, as it depends on finding whipworm eggs in the feces. It can be difficult to control whipworm eggs on grass or soil, but concrete and tile can be effectively disinfected. To prevent exposure, any feces in the yard should be picked up on a daily basis. Consult with your veterinarian for treatment and control of whipworm.

Tapeworm

Dogs can carry several types of tapeworm, and they can acquire them from eating infected fleas (or more rarely, lice). They make their home in the canine intestine but are also transmissible to people. Infected dogs may appear quite normal, and you probably won't even know your pet is affected unless you notice the rice-like segments of the worms on your dog's feces or near his anus. Your vet can prescribe a special dewormer to rid your dog of them.

Blastomycosis

Blastomyces dermatitidis, or "blasto," is a pathogenic fungus that can cause skin and respiratory infections in both dogs and people. It can also infect other organ systems. This fungus exists as a mold in the environment and becomes a yeast at body temperature. It is most common in the acidic soils of the midwest and central southern areas in the United States. Young male hunting Beagles are most at risk because they are most likely to become active in that environment. Dogs who spend time around the water are even more vulnerable, and even a brief exposure can lead to infection.

Dogs become infected only through direct contact with mold spores, either by inhaling them or by having an open wound through which the invisible spores enter the body (as when your Beagle rolls in contaminated soil). Once the spores enter the lungs, they become yeast that multiply like mad. The resulting skin lesions may not show up for weeks after the infection.

Blasto infects multiple organs. If the infection occurs through the skin, the dog develops wet, itchy lesions that if left untreated can damage nearby muscle and bone tissue. Even more serious (and more common) is pneumonia developing from respiratory infections. Infected dogs cough, lose their appetite, develop pneumonia, and may die if untreated. Luckily, the disease is treatable with new antifungal drugs, especially if caught early. (Be warned—these medications are expensive but necessary.) Eighty-five percent of dogs with mild forms of the disease who are treated early will survive.

There is no real way to prevent your Beagle from coming down with this disease, although it will help to avoid known blasto "hot spots" and attempt to keep your dog from digging as much as possible. Unfortunately, soil testing is not reliable, and if the stuff is in your yard, you can't get rid of it.

Heartworm

The heartworm is a long, slender worm that passes from mosquitoes to your dog in the larval stage. The larvae enter the bloodstream and wind up in the heart, where they continue to develop into adult worms. The adults produce larvae that circulate in the blood. Their life cycle is pretty complicated, because these new larvae can't grow into adults until they are ingested by a second mosquito, where they molt and are redeposited into another (or even the same) dog. The blood contains microscopic heartworm babies. Once inside the dog, the baby heartworms can grow into truly hideous adults over a foot long. The disease causes serious irreversible damage to the heart, the lungs, and the arteries feeding them.

Heartworm is present throughout most of the United States, especially in areas with warmer climates. Over 244,000 dogs test positive for infection each year. The only way to tell if your dog has heartworm is for him to be checked by a vet. She can perform a simple blood test for heartworm, which will detect the presence of the worm before any symptoms appear. If the disease is more advanced, your dog may cough, lose weight, or experience heart failure.

The treatment for heartworm is arduous for the dog and expensive for you; however, it's great to know that the disease is easily prevented. Heartworm prevention is safer and easier than treatment, and it should be started by the time your dog is 12 weeks old. Many kinds of heartworm preventions also protect against intestinal parasites or even fleas. Check with your vet to see what plan is right for your

On very rare occasions, humans have been known to harbor heartworms. The infant heartworms are transferred to people through mosquitoes but can't follow their normal life cycle. Instead of invading the cardiac and pulmonary arteries, they end up as cysts in the lungs or inside the eye.

Health of Your Beagle 145

dog. A once-a-month prescription tablet or topical treatment will do the trick. Discuss your options with your veterinarian. Regardless of which preventative you choose, however, it's important that the dog be tested for heartworm first. The medication causes the death of any heartworms in the body, and if a dog is heartworm positive, the sudden death of the worms could clog his arteries and kill him.

Ringworm

Despite the name, ringworm is not a worm but a transmissible fungal infection usually characterized by circular hair loss and scaly skin. It is not usually itchy. Most cases disappear by themselves, but more severe cases can be treated with antifungal medications.

If your dog gets ringworm, have him (and all the other dogs and cats in your home) treated, and then clean your house thoroughly. This includes getting the air filters changed and disinfecting animal bedding, brushes, and combs with bleach. Ringworm spores can float around in the air for years.

Giardia

Giardia is a single-celled (protozoal) parasite that lives in the small intestine of any mammal, including humans. Giardia has two life stages: the cyst and the trophozoite. Dogs can become infected if they drink cyst-contaminated water, lick cyst-contaminated feces, or devour cyst-infected

Dogs can become infected with giardia if they drink cyst-contaminated water.

prey. When the giardia enter the dog's gastrointestinal system, they enter a new phase of life and reproduce rapidly.

The main signs of giardiasis are vomiting and diarrhea. Infected humans report cramping and nausea also, but these symptoms are difficult to detect in dogs. If the condition is not treated, infected animals can suffer weight loss and continued periods of vomiting and diarrhea. A stool sample is sometimes used for diagnosis, although even that can be hit or miss. A blood test known as the ELISA blood test is more accurate, because it looks for a specific protein particular to giardia. This test is quite a bit more expensive than the fecal test, however. Several drugs are available to treat giardiasis, and there is also a vaccine available. Discuss these options with your vet.

Coccidia

Coccidiosis is an intestinal disease that affects several different animals, including canines and humans. The susceptibility to this infection is quite variable, and diagnosis is difficult. The disease is often considered opportunistic, meaning it develops when other stress factors are present. Beagles seem rather prone to coccidia, possibly because of increased exposure; many Beagles spend a lot of time outdoors hunting. Young males are most likely affected, and it seems to be more prevalent in the western part of the United States. This condition is very rare in the United Kingdom, however. Signs of coccidiosis usually appear around such events as a change in weather, weaning, overcrowding, long trips, relocation, or unsanitary conditions. "Nervous coccidiosis" is a nervous system condition associated with coccidial infection. Dogs can die from serious cases, either from the disease itself or from secondary diseases such as pneumonia.

Currently, there is no medication that will kill coccidian—we have to leave that up to the dog's own immune system! However, there are some medications called "coccidiostats" that inhibit coccidial reproduction and make it easier for the immune system to do its work. A typical treatment course lasts about a week or two, but sometimes courses as long as a month are needed.

COMMON DISORDERS AND DISEASES

Although many diseases will be discussed in this chapter, don't worry. Your Beagle won't get them all, or even most of them. He may not get any of them, and he may very well live to the ripe old age of 20 or so. However, most dogs do contract some type of health problem sooner or later, and many of the diseases described below are some for which Beagles are more at risk than other breeds.

Allergies

An allergic reaction occurs when the immune system overreacts to an otherwise innocuous substance, like pollen or grass. The offending substance is called an allergen. Usually, a dog shows no response when he is first exposed to an allergen, because the immune system is building up a reserve of antibodies. The next time the dog encounters that same allergen, the immune system reacts strongly. Dogs who become allergic usually do so in the first three or four years of life, although if their owner moves to a new area with new

Keeping your dog parasite free will help prevent allergies. Here's why: As the immune system develops antibodies to parasites like fleas, mites, intestinal worms, and heartworms, it may also develop sensitivities to other otherwise harmless substances in the environment.

allergens, an older dog (especially one with previous allergies) may develop new ones.

Combinations of allergens can have an additive effect, with more severe signs. Thus, a dog allergic to both pollen and ragweed will have worse symptoms than one allergic to ragweed alone. Dogs are often sensitive to the same allergens that annoy humans, but dogs respond differently because the route of exposure and biochemistry of the reaction is different in the two species: Humans usually sneeze, while dogs usually scratch. It appears that liver, lemon, and blue Beagles have more problems with allergies than tricolors, although this hasn't officially been studied.

An itchy dog can be tested for allergies through blood tests; high amounts of a certain antibody, called IgE, usually indicate a hypersensitivity to an allergen. Also, to diagnose what may be causing the problem, a veterinary allergist may do some skin testing. The dog is sedated and small injections of the suspected substances are administered. Reactions are recorded 15 to 20 minutes afterward.

Unfortunately, allergies cannot be cured, although they are treatable. Treatment may include food, supplements, or capsules containing essential fatty acids; antihistamines (often used in conjunction with essential fatty acids); steroids (although side effects may outweigh benefits); and hyposensitizing vaccines (effective about 60 percent of the time; they take about nine months to become effective). Avoidance of the allergen is the best therapy, but it's not usually possible.

Basic Signs of Illness

While every disease is unique, there are some general ways in which they manifest themselves. The savvy dog owner is aware of them. To know when to go to the vet is tricky, but it's best to err on the side of caution. Your dog can't vocalize how he feels when something is wrong, and he may suffer for days before he actually starts showing signs. If you suspect that your Beagle is not feeling well, take him to the veterinarian right away. The following are some signs that your Beagle may be feeling under the weather:

- Vomiting
- Diarrhea
- Constipation
- Runny eyes or nose
- Excessive panting
- Itching

- Changes in normal activity level
- Lumps and bumps
- Hair loss
- Pain when touched
- Limping

Atopic Dermatitis

Atopic dermatitis is an allergic skin disease caused by hypersensitivity to common substances in the environment, like house dust mites. These creatures live in all of our houses in rugs, bedding, sofas, and other soft furnishings, and they feed on skin scales that are constantly falling from people and animals.

Atopic dermatitis often first becomes apparent in the first two years of life. You may notice your Beagle licking himself excessively, especially his paws, abdomen, face, "armpit," and perineum. His ears may be reddened and even hot to the touch, and smelly yeast infections of the ear may also occur. Hot spots may even strike, and while they may be seemingly independent problems, they are actually part of the same disease. As the disease progresses, baldness and skin infections become common. With long-standing problems, the skin itself may change color, with a black mottling developing on the abdomen.

Food Allergies

In dogs, the most common causes of adverse reactions are beef, dairy products, wheat, chicken, and pork, in approximately that order. It may take months for a dog to develop an allergy to any particular food. Because some sort of protein is usually the culprit, you may need to feed your Beagle a protein source that he has not eaten before, a so-called "novel protein." Popular ones include duck, salmon, and whitefish. In certain cases, you may find your dog is allergic to *all* of these protein sources, in which case he may need a special diet with specially broken-down proteins. See your veterinarian for more information and options.

Itching

Itching is caused by certain chemical reactions that occur in the skin and stimulate the nerves. Like everyone else, a dog has an itch threshold, which is the point at which he simply must scratch. Itching can be caused by a host of conditions, including secondary bacterial skin infections (pyoderma), allergies (pollens, house dust mites, molds, certain foods, or contact allergy to something that actually touches the skin), or skin parasites (sarcoptic or demodectic mange, fleas, cheyletiella mites, ear mites, or lice). Many of these conditions also manifest themselves as licking of the feet. If itching or licking occurs, you need to find out what is causing the problem. Your veterinarian can help you.

The most common causes of food allergies in dogs are beef, dairy products, wheat, chicken, and pork.

Beagle Pain Syndrome (BPS)

Beagle Pain Syndrome (BPS), or necrotizing vasculitis, is a complex condition involving sterile meningitis and polyarteritis (the simultaneous inflammation of a number of arteries). Polyarteritis describes a disorder in which a large number of arteries become inflamed, while meningitis is the inflammations of the meninges. (Sterile meningitis is not infective.) This condition is not well understood, not even by most veterinarians. It is generally first noted in puppies from four to ten months of age but can be seen in older dogs of either sex. An immune-mediated basis, probably hereditary, is suspected. Left untreated, the first episode may resolve within a few days, but a relapse will probably occur within a few months. Signs include:

- neck pain and stiffness
- shaking
- hunchback stance
- fever
- lack of appetite
- muscle spasms (especially in the front legs and neck)
- lethargy
- reluctance to move or bark

Treatment with prednisone for short-term therapy has been suggested, and long-term treatment with lower dosages may be indicated for some Beagles. Your veterinarian will help you decide what the best course of therapy is. Steroid treatment will make your Beagle drink more water and may cause water retention. More frequent potty breaks are usually needed, and you should keep your Beagle in a quiet, nonstimulating environment. Remember that moving can be painful, so if you have an active household with kids and other dogs, confine your Beagle in a crate or separate area.

Bone and Joint Disorders

Most dogs will develop some kind of joint disease during their lives that will usually appear as they grow older. Signs of joint disease include stiffness, limping, or favoring a limb. You may notice your dog's reluctance to climb stairs, jump, or even get up. Causes of such pain can include arthritis, dysplasia, Lyme disease, intervertebral disk disease, tendon or muscle disease, fractures, and obesity.

Arthritis

As our dogs live longer lives, they are at increased risk of developing arthritis. About 20 percent of all adult dogs have arthritis to some degree, and obese individuals who carry the most weight are more likely to be affected. For dogs (and people), the most common type of arthritis is osteoarthritis, which results from damaged cartilage. Because cartilage doesn't have nerves, the dog feels no pain and continues to be active. This only accelerates the damage. Signs of arthritis include:

- Avoidance of activity
- Limping

- Reluctance to get up or climb stairs
- Sensitivity to cold and damp weather
- Shrinking away from being touched
- Stiffness

Arthritis can be more troublesome to dogs than blindness or deafness, but we have ways to combat it. Many new medications can make a positive difference in your dog's life. Nutraceuticals, a new class of supplements between regular drugs and traditional herbal preparations, offer important benefits to arthritic dogs. Examples include glucosamine and chondroitin. Glucosamine is a cartilage-protective nutraceutical, while chondroitin sulfate is an important glycoaminoglycan (GAG) that binds water in the cartilage matrix. Adding both glucosamine and chondroitin sulfate in a single supplement is a great way to help your pet heal himself. These supplements are not simply "painkillers." Their direct effect is to be both protective and restorative, leading to less pain and more mobility. This, in turn, will have an important effect on your dog's attitude. It is important to remember, however, that unlike traditional drug therapy, nutraceuticals work slowly (six to eight weeks), and not all dogs respond. Make sure you buy a high-quality supplement, as not all are created equal. Check with your veterinarian as well before buying something over the counter.

Other treatments that have been found to be effective against arthritis include physical therapy, Chinese or Japanese acupuncture, chiropractic treatment, and even gene therapy. There's a whole new world out there for arthritis sufferers, and your logy, creaky, slow-to-get-up and hesitant-to-climb-stairs dog may get a new lease on life with one of the many new treatments available. So far, though, there is no real cure for arthritis—only relief from its more debilitating effects. In addition to veterinary care, you can make your Beagle more comfortable at home by supplying extra bedding and a snug place by the fire or hot air vent.

Cleft Lip or Cleft Palate

Dogs with this condition have a fissure or cleft in the roof of the mouth or upper lip. A congenital hereditary condition, it allows food and fluid to enter the nasal-respiratory pathway, which can result in suffocation or inhalation pneumonia. It is a congenital hereditary condition, and the only treatment available is surgery.

Beagle Dwarfism

Beagles can suffer from various forms of inherited skeletal dysplasias resulting in dwarfism. These include "funny puppy syndrome" and Chinese Beagle syndrome. In the dog world, dwarfism is considered a disorder that reduces the size of a dog below that which is reasonably established as expected for a given breed. Some kinds of dwarfism include physical deformities, while others do not. For example, Beagle "funny puppies" are the runts of the litter who seem slower to develop than their littermates. Many seem to suffer extreme pain at about three weeks of age and are unable to bear weight on one foreleg. This passes, but about a week later, more problems may appear, with the dog unable to walk well. By four to six months of age, the condition stabilizes, although at this point the dog will have a roached back, crooked legs, and limp. Many also feature a bad bite and other dental problems, as well as certain other deformities. Despite these problems, these dogs are tremendously loving, smart, and affectionate.

Another form of dwarfism is Chinese Beagle syndrome, so-called because of the wide skull and slanted eyes manifested by many of its sufferers. These dogs have apparently normal bone and joint development, although they move stiffly, with some dogs unable to flex their pasterns. The problem seems to be that the cells in the kidney and bone are unable to respond to normal amounts of the parathyroid hormone. There may also be associated neurological and heart problems. Despite all of this, most Chinese Beagles seem to live a normal life.

Hip Dysplasia

Dysplasia means "developmental abnormality," and dogs with this condition have an abnormal formation of the hip socket, causing rear limb lameness. It is not as common in Beagles as in some larger breeds, but it can appear. Fortunately, there are several kinds of surgeries available to correct this condition.

Elbow Dysplasia

Elbow dysplasia is the forelimb counterpart to hip dysplasia, but unlike hip dysplasia, it has only been recognized as a problem during the past few decades. Elbow dysplasia can take four different forms, and a dog might have just one or all four of these! Dogs with elbow dysplasia are lame in one or both front legs. There is surgery to correct the problem, should it appear, but the dog needs cage rest for four to six weeks afterward. That is the toughest part! Fortunately, elbow dysplasia is not too common in Beagles.

Dogs with elbow dysplasia are lame in one or both front legs.

Herniated Disk and Intervertebral Disk Disease

Both Beagles and humans can suffer from a herniated disk that can lead to paralysis. This disease is relatively common in Beagles of both sexes. In dogs who suffer from intervertebral disk disease (a hereditary condition), there is a dorsal rupture of the disks between the vertebral bodies. It generally occurs at about one year of age.

Between each pair of vertebrae there is an intervertebral disk that in many ways is similar to a jelly doughnut. There's an outside part, the annulus fibrosis, and an inner, jelly-like, shock-absorbing part, the nucleus pulposus. If the jelly gets hard, it can no longer act as a shock absorber. Then, if too much pressure is put on it, the calcified jelly-like material can burst out against the spinal cord. This is called a herniation, and the pressure against the spine can cause paralysis. The place where the herniation occurs will determine the kind of injury. If the herniation occurs low in the back, only the hind limbs will be affected. If it occurs higher up, it could affect all four legs. If this happens to your Beagle, the faster you seek medical attention, the better his chances are for a full recovery. The first signs are usually a loss of "proprioception," which means the dog can no longer feel where his limbs are. (He will stand with his paws in strange positions and may not try to set them right if you place them in an odd way.) The second stage is "ataxia," characterized by a drunken-like walk. From there, it only gets worse.

In mild cases, rest may bring the dog back to normal. If not, decompression surgery is usually suggested. The vet may recommend diagnostic imaging first to be sure where the problem has occurred. The surgery is effective in about 90 percent of cases if done promptly. (Although people experience slipped disks, the condition is much more serious in dogs, as a rule.) However, a new study at Purdue University holds out hope. After administering a liquid polymer called polyethylene glycol (PEG), researchers found that more than 70 percent of dogs recovered use of their legs if treated within 72 hours. And they recovered extremely quickly. Human beings may be trying it out next!

Physical therapy is also recommended for dogs with herniated disks, whether they have surgery or not. Unfortunately, once a dog experiences a herniated disk, his chances of reoccurrence increase. The best thing you can do to prevent this from happening is to keep your dog fit and lean, give him daily moderate exercise, and use a harness rather than a collar in order to relieve some of the pressure on his neck.

Luxation of the Patella (Knee)

Patellar luxation (slipped kneecap) affects the hind limbs. The patella lies in a groove at the lower end of the femur. Dogs with this hereditary condition don't have the proper structure holding the knee in place, and the knee swivels inward. Another way of thinking about it is that the quadriceps (the big muscle on the thigh) is actually pulling the wrong way. In rarer cases, a slipped kneecap can result from trauma. It generally occurs when the animal is under one year of age.

A dog with patellar luxation usually doesn't appear to be hurting. In fact, he may seem normal one moment and hopping around the next. Other signs include difficulty in fully bending the rear leg and kicking the leg out behind—that's how the dog tries to pop the knee back into place. It is definitely diagnosed by an x-ray or through palpation of the joint by the vet.

The condition can be repaired surgically, but there's nothing you can do to prevent it. Patellar luxation comes in four "grades," and if left uncorrected, Grade 2 or higher can result in severe lameness as the kneecap keeps slipping.

Cancer

Cancer is an uncontrolled growth of cells on or inside the body. It can occur in almost any organ or body system. Some cancers are localized, affecting only one organ, while others spread to adjacent tissues. Dogs get cancer at roughly the same rate as humans, and like humans, the rate increases with age. No one knows exactly why cancer occurs, and most kinds are difficult to prevent, although spaying a female before her first heat cycle will greatly reduce her risk of mammary cancer. Every different kind of cancer requires a different kind of treatment and has a different prognosis.

If discovered early enough, most forms of cancer can be treated or even cured by surgery, chemotherapy, radiation therapy, or a combination of the three. Therefore, keep an eye out for the traditional signs of cancer:

- A lump that seems to be increasing in size, especially one that seems hard or attached to the bone.
- A sore that doesn't heal.
- Changes in elimination habits, such as chronic diarrhea or difficulty eliminating.
- Bleeding from any body opening.
- Loss of appetite or unexplained weight loss.
- Difficulty breathing.
- Persistent lameness.

Cancer does not have to be hopeless. Many cases, especially if caught early, can be successfully treated with surgery, radiation, chemotherapy, or a combination of all three. The very word "chemotherapy" strikes fear into the hearts of some dog owners, but perhaps it shouldn't. Fortunately, dogs seldom have the nausea or hair loss that is often a side effect of chemotherapy in humans. One reason for this is that the chemo used for dogs is much milder than for people. In human chemotherapy, doctors may use as many as ten different drugs. In animal chemo, though, usually only three are used. This is because cancer is usually fairly well developed in dogs by the time it is discovered, and so the goal is not to cure the disease; rather, it is to lengthen

Dogs who live in a home with human smokers have an increased risk of cancer, just as humans do.

and enhance the quality of life for the animal. Radiation treatment, on the other hand, affects dogs and humans pretty much the same way. It is generally used for cancers that do not respond to surgery or chemo.

Nutrition can help, too. Feed a food with increased fatty acids, proteins, and fats. This type of diet will help meet the added energy requirements of the cancer patient and may counteract both the effects of cancer and the side effects of cancer therapy.

The following are some of the more common cancers affecting Beagles.

Lymphoma

Lymphoma is a common cancer that can affect the liver, lungs, or digestive system, and its signs vary according to what organ is first affected. Lethargy, vomiting, yellowing of the gums, and coughing can all be warning signs. Beagles are at higher risk for this condition than most other breeds, and most cases occur in middle-aged dogs (six to seven years old). Chemotherapy or prednisone are often used to treat lymphoma. There is news on this front, however. A researcher at Colorado State University has developed a test capable of detecting lymphoma in dogs before clinical signs are evident. Stay tuned.

Skin Cancer

Skin cancer is a broad term that covers any tumors of the skin and its associated structures (glands, hair follicles, and connective tissue). This is the most common kind of cancer in dogs. Most victims are over the age of six, although certain types occur in younger animals, too. The cause for most types of cancer is unknown, although exposure to sunlight plays a role in two types (squamous cell carcinoma and

Physical Therapy

Physical therapy is becoming established in veterinary medicine, not only for post-operative patients but for geriatric dogs, arthritic dogs, obese animals, and canine athletes. Before therapy is begun, a complete orthopedic and neurological examination is performed to see what therapy is needed and what improvement can be expected. Equipment includes physioballs, balance boards, treadmills (both land and underwater), and ultrasound equipment to break down abnormal adhesions between tissues. And yes, plain old-fashioned exercise is used as well.

hemangioma). You can't diagnose skin cancer yourself from harmless lumps and benign tumors, so report any suspicious lumps to your veterinarian for a thorough checkup. This may include a fine needle aspirate to examine cells, a complete blood count, serum chemistry panel, urinalysis, and chest x-rays (to see if the tumor has spread to the lungs). Treatment for skin cancer will vary depending its type and stage. It may include surgery, radiation therapy, chemotherapy, cryosurgery (freezing), and photodynamic therapy.

Cardiovascular Disease

About 3.2 million dogs in the United States show some form of acquired heart disease. Unfortunately, early stages have no visible signs, although careful examination by a vet may uncover some of them. A stethoscope can reveal murmurs and fluid in the lungs; palpation can reveal unusual pulses; radiographs show enlargement of the heart; an EKG can identify heart enlargement and irregular rhythms; and blood and urine tests can reveal heartworms and the condition of other internal organs.

Like people, dogs can get heart disease. Sometimes it is present at birth (congenital), while sometimes it develops later in life. The latter is more common, and it affects many older dogs. In one type of acquired heart disease, the heart valves lose their ability to close properly; this causes abnormal blood flow. In another type, the walls of the heart

Extreme lethargy may be a sign that your Beagle is not feeling well.

become thin and weak. Both types can cause heart failure, a condition in which the heart cannot pump blood at the rate the body demands. As the heart works harder and harder to pump blood throughout the body, more damage can result. Fluids build up in the body, and sodium and water are retained, a condition called congestive heart failure. Dogs of any age can develop heart failure. Signs of heart failure include coughing, shortness of breath, difficult breathing, weight loss, and fatigue.

Treatment for congestive heart failure may include diuretics, nitroglycerine, drainage of the fluid around the lungs, an angiotensin-converting enzyme inhibitor, a low sodium diet, and the drug digoxin. Your veterinarian will help you decide what treatment is best for your Beagle.

Dental Disease

While teeth are obviously important to dogs, a recent survey noted that only one out of ten owners gives their dog proper dental care. It's true that dogs seldom get cavities; however, the plaque and tartar that collects on the teeth can cause gingivitis and periodontal disease, leading to tooth decay, bleeding gums, and tooth loss. Affecting 85 percent of dogs by age four, periodontal disease is the most frequently diagnosed health problem in pets. Even worse, the responsible bacteria can travel through the bloodstream and eventually damage the heart and other major organs. An unhealthy mouth usually indicates an unhealthy body. Signs of dental problems include:

- Yellow-brown crust on teeth
- Bleeding gums
- Bad breath
- Tooth loss
- Subdued behavior
- Abnormal drooling
- Dropping food from the mouth or swallowing it whole
- Approaching the food bowl but not eating

Normal dry kibble provides some dental benefit because of its crunchy effect plus the moderate scraping action that it provides. However, specially formulated foods are available that can do a much better job of cleaning your Beagle's teeth. Ask your veterinarian for help in selecting the best food for your pet.

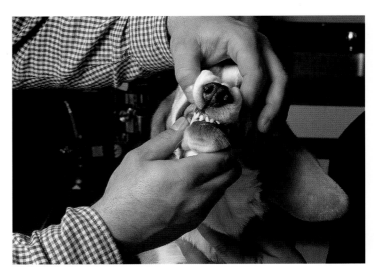

Regular dental examinations are crucial to the prevention of dental disease in your Beagle.

Halitosis (Bad Breath)

Believe it or not, dog breath is not supposed to smell bad. In the best-case scenario, it may mean he's been eating something rather nasty, but if the smell doesn't go away (even after you brush your dog's teeth), it may signal dental disease or the presence of a foreign body that's stuck in there. A metabolic condition called ketoacidosis can also produce a fruity odor to the breath. Bad breath can also be a sign of diabetes, kidney disease, gastrointestinal disease, infections around the mouth, respiratory problems, dietary indiscretions, tonsillitis, or mouth and gum disease.

In most cases, the cure for bad breath is a thorough professional teeth cleaning, which will take care of or at least halt the progression of some of the underlying problems.

Digestive Disorders

Like all dogs, Beagles are prone to a number of gastrointestinal conditions, including inflammatory bowel disease, pancreatitis, vomiting, constipation, and diarrhea.

Inflammatory Bowel Disease (IBD)

This is a condition characterized by mucous-like diarrhea and vomiting. It is triggered by certain inflammatory cells that invade the stomach or intestine. When the stomach is affected, vomiting is more common; when the intestines are affected, the dog will experience diarrhea. Both the diarrhea and vomiting can be intermittent. No one yet knows exactly why dogs come down with this disease, although factors include genetics, nutrition, problems with the immune system, and sometimes infection.

The only definitive way to diagnose inflammatory bowel disease is through a biopsy, which will reveal increased numbers of inflammatory cells in the intestinal wall. (The biopsy can be done through an endoscope by exploratory surgery.) Once diagnosed, IBD may respond to nutritional therapy and various medications. The vet will probably put the dog on a special food trial, which includes a novel protein and carbohydrate source (one your dog has probably never eaten, like emu and potatoes). The dog can eat nothing else for two to three months. If that doesn't work, a high-fiber, lower-fat diet may be tried. In any case, carbohydrates with glutens (wheat, oats, rye, and barley) are best avoided. Some vets recommend the addition of omega-3 fatty acids to decrease the inflammation of the GI tract as well.

Medication is also an important part of treating the disease, which can be controlled but not cured. Your vet can discuss various options with you.

Pancreatitis

The pancreas serves many functions in the body, and one of them is to produces enzymes that help digest food by exporting enzymes to the intestine, where they become activated. In dogs who suffer from pancreatitis, the enzymes become activated in the pancreas itself or at some other stage before delivery to the intestines.

The origin is frequently unknown, although diet is a major cause of the disease, particularly a high-fat meal like ham (or a meal of garbage). Hormonal diseases like Cushing's disease can also bring it on, as can infections or trauma. The disease is notoriously hard to diagnose—only a biopsy can tell you for sure.

There's no easy cure for pancreatitis. Treatment involves fasting, fluid therapy, and medication to calm the inflammation. It's actually easier to prevent than to treat this disease, which is why it's so important to feed your dog healthy foods.

Vomiting

Because dogs are scavengers by nature, nature has provided them with an easy way to rid themselves of a bad digestive experience—throwing up. If vomiting occurs once, it's probably nothing to worry about, but repeated vomiting is a sign of trouble, and you should take your dog to the vet. In fact, continued vomiting can signal a metabolic or digestive problem, infections, or even heartworm. If your pet begins to vomit, take note and examine the vomit. Note the color (red, yellow, black, etc), and see if it contains undigested food or just liquid. Your vet needs to know all of this. In some cases, he may even want a sample.

Constipation

A constipated dog has infrequent or difficult evacuation of the stool. The feces are usually hard and dry. Causes can include insufficient fiber or water in the diet, impacted bone or other foreign materials that form hard masses, insufficient exercise, aging, fracture of the pelvic limbs, prostate disease, tumors, spine or disk disease, or certain endocrine disorders. Proper treatment requires finding the underlying cause and rectifying it. Causes can vary from

Some gastrointestinal disorders may be brought on by contaminated food or water.

impaction of the bowel from eating bones to diseases like an enlarged prostate gland or a perineal hernia. Always make sure your dog has access to plenty of fresh water, and ensure that he has frequent opportunities to eliminate. In some cases, a high-fiber diet may help, but check with your vet. Sometimes the opposite kind of diet (low residue, high digestibility) will achieve better results.

Diarrhea

Like vomiting, a single incident of diarrhea is not a big deal. However, prolonged diarrhea can be dangerous. It can be caused by bacteria, viruses, parasites, stress, toxins, organ dysfunction, or even a change in diet. Diarrhea in puppies is much more serious than in adults, as puppies can quickly become dehydrated and even die.

Even if it doesn't signal another more serious condition, diarrhea can produce a loss of electrolytes that in turn can lead to pancreatitis or inflammation. Take note of the diarrhea; examine its color (red, yellow, or black) and check whether or not it is tinged with mucus. (These are important diagnostic tools for your vet.)

Diarrhea may also be classified as acute (sudden onset and of brief duration) or chronic (long term). Acute diarrhea of the small intestine usually lasts less than 48 hours. The stools are brown or reddish brown and may

Diarrhea can have its source from either the small intestine or the large intestine, in which case it's called colitis. Colitis is most frequently causes by whipworms, tumors or polyps, dietary changes, allergies, or inappropriately swallowed objects.

contain blood but seldom mucus. One of the downsides to owning a dog is that you have to pay attention to this kind of stuff. The dog may also lose his appetite. If the diarrhea continues for seven to ten days (or more), it is labeled as chronic. Diarrhea of the large intestine usually contains lot of mucus.

Loose stools could just mean that your pet ate a meal that didn't agree with his system. Prolonged diarrhea, on the other hand, can create a loss of electrolytes that could lead to other serious problems, like diabetes, distemper, pancreatitis, infection, inflammation, or cancer. If the diarrhea continues for more than a day, take your dog to the vet. He will probably ask you to fast your Beagle for a day or two (although you should continue to give water as a rule). Your vet will also ask for a fecal sample, and in serious cases may want do a biopsy. Severely dehydrated pets may need IV fluids.

Dogs with diarrhea often do well on a diet with a moderate amount of highly digestible protein (as from eggs or cottage cheese), with no more than 15 percent fat. If you add a carbohydrate, make it rice.

Change in Appetite

Decreased appetite could be as simple as a stomach ache or as serious as cancer. A sudden increase in appetite may also be significant, especially if it's not accompanied by weight gain. And if your dog suddenly develops pica, a penchant for eating nonfood items, that could mean something as well. Note these symptoms and talk to your vet. Unexplained weight loss also warrants a trip to the vet.

Ear Infections

Ear trouble can be very serious in Beagles. Ears not only enable a dog to hear, but they enable him to keep his balance. Dog ears are structured differently from human ears in an important way. Instead of having a direct, horizontal passage from the outer to the inner ear, the dog ear makes an L-shaped turn. This shape may help protect a dog's middle and inner ear from injury, but it also allows a pileup of wax, dirt, and infective debris at the turn.

Like most dogs with generous, hanging ears, Beagles are vulnerable to ear infections. These infections usually develop because the moist environment of the ears makes a comfortable, home-like environment for yeast and bacteria. The Beagle's ears hang down and cover the ear canal, preventing air from circulating and drying the area. To help keep your Beagle's ears healthy, examine them often and

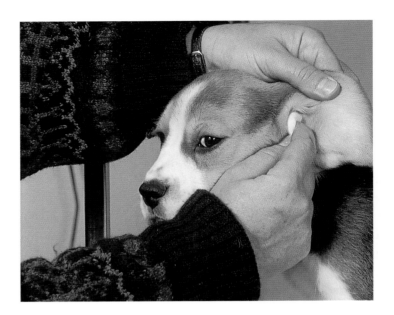

To help keep your Beagle's ears healthy, examine and clean them often.

make sure the canal is clean. Ear infections usually have a characteristic foul, yeasty, or fruity odor. Wipe away debris with cotton balls without digging too deep. (You don't want to damage the eardrum.) You should also clean them after your dog has been swimming.

The most common ear infection is called otitis externa, infection of the outer ear, but if it isn't treated correctly, it can migrate into the middle or even the inner ear, which is much worse. The first signs may be an unpleasant odor, redness, swelling, or discharge. Other signs include scratching, shaking, rubbing of the ears or head, pain around the ears, and behavioral changes. You should contact your vet at the first sign of an ear infection. Most cases can be treated with a combination of antibacterial and antifungal agents; however, unless the underlying cause is treated, the infection will return.

Endocrine System Disorders

The endocrine system produces the hormones that keep the body running right. When this system goes awry, the results can be devastating.

Diabetes Mellitus

Diabetes mellitus (sugar diabetes) is a common disease in Beagles, as it is in human beings. Females are affected twice as often as males. It is caused by a lower than normal production of insulin. (This can be influenced by factors such as obesity, genetic predisposition, poor diet, stress, and certain drugs.) Insulin is produced in the islet cells of the pancreas. It controls blood glucose concentrations or blood sugar, the body's main fuel. Dogs with diabetes have a chronic elevation of blood sugar. This eventually reaches the point where the glucose leaks into the urine, taking more water with it. The excessive loss of water in urine is then compensated for by increased thirst and subsequent water consumption.

Diabetes comes in two forms: Type I and Type II. Type I is the most serious and the one that most often affects dogs. Beagles are reported to be at increased risk for Type I compared to many other breeds, with the incidence peaking at between seven and nine years of age.

There is no cure for Type I or Type II diabetes. Treatment requires providing a controlled diet, proper exercise, and daily injected insulin therapy. Each diabetic animal has to have his insulin dose tailored to his individual needs, which is done over a stabilization period. Diabetic dogs need to have a constant diet, so it's best to use commercially produced rather than homecooked diets, which can vary in sugar content. In fact, even many commercial foods have nutritional profiles that can vary from batch to batch.

Thyroid Problems

The thyroid is a small but important butterfly-shaped gland lying just below the larynx. It is comprised of two lobes and has a very important role in your dog's health. It works with the hypothalamus and pituitary gland (both located in the brain) to regulate the body's metabolism.

Beagles seem predisposed to various thyroid conditions, including hypothyroidism and thyroid cancers. They are also candidates for Addison's disease (hyperadrenocorticism) and Cushing's disease (hypoadrenocorticism). In Beagles, most victims are middle-aged and older.

- **Hypothyroidism:** Hypothyroidism is the most common hormonal disorder in dogs who are between four and ten years of age, although it often crops up during puberty. As its name indicates, hypothyroidism is a disorder of the thyroid gland, which is located in the neck. The thyroid gland produces the hormone thyroxine, which regulates the metabolic rate in many different tissues. In dogs who are suffering from hypothyroidism, not enough thyroxine is produced, which causes the metabolism in these tissues to slow down. Most cases result from an immune-mediated process that develops in genetically susceptible dogs.

Signs of hypothyroidism include lethargy, depression, exercise intolerance, obesity, digestive disorders, cold intolerance, and skin disorders, especially a thin, harsh coat with symmetrical hair loss.

Diagnosis can be complicated, involving a complete blood count, chemistry panel, urinalysis, thyroxine level test, or a thyroid stimulating hormone (TSH) test. Treatment is usually just a daily oral dose of synthetic thyroxine, which must be continued for the rest of the dog's life.

- **Addison's Disease (Hypoadrenocorticism):** One of the most common diseases of the endocrine system is Addison's disease (hypoadrenocorticism), which affects the adrenal glands, found right next to the kidneys. The center (cortex) of the gland produces a group of special hormones called corticosteroids, which include mineralocorticoids such as aldosterone. These handy hormones help mammals adapt to stress. In fact, one subcategory of them, the glucocorticoids (like cortisol), are responsible for producing that all-important flight-or-flight response. Other kinds of hormones produced by the adrenal glands help balance electrolytes (sodium, potassium, and chloride) in the system. As a result, when something goes awry with the adrenal glands, your pet is in big trouble!

The typical Addison's patient is a female aged four to five years, although any dog of any age may be affected. Signs may include lethargy, lack of appetite, vomiting, or diarrhea, but they are vague, intermittent, and various. This is one reason that Addison's is called "the great imitator." Your vet needs to perform a special test called the ACTH stimulation test to be sure.

If left unnoticed or untreated, your dog will experience an "Addisonian crisis" in which his blood sugar will drop dangerously low and the imbalance of electrolytes will disrupt the heart rhythm. Untreated dogs usually die. Fortunately, the disease can be managed with medications. Treatment includes replacing the missing mineralocorticoid hormones. Your vet will be able to prescribe the right medication for your particular dog, but in any case, he must remain on it for life. Common medications for Addison's include low-dose prednisone (to replace the cortisone). The aldosterone can be replaced by a daily oral medication or a monthly injectable. The injectable medication is less expensive than the oral treatment, but neither is cheap. Addison's dogs need careful monitoring, and if they receive it, they can live a full and fairly normal life.

- **Cushing's Disease (Hyperadrenocorticism):** This disease is caused by the production of too much adrenal hormone, specifically corticosteroids. In some cases, the precipitating cause is a tumor either in the adrenal gland itself or more commonly in the pituitary gland, which stimulates the adrenal gland to produce hormones. Beagles are more prone to this condition than some other breeds.

Signs of Cushing's disease include excessive thirst, increased urination, panting, symmetrical hair loss, skin infections, and high blood pressure. Several blood tests are used to diagnose the disease, notably the low-dose dexamethasone test. Once the disease is diagnosed, the high-dose dexamethasone suppression test is performed to distinguish the kind of tumor involved. An adrenal gland tumor

Some diseases, like Addison's disease, may be treated with an injectable medication.

can sometimes be removed, but pituitary tumors are generally left in place. The disease is then treated (but not cured) with mitotane, the dosage of which must be carefully regulated.

Eye Disorders

All breeds of dog can suffer from eye diseases, and Beagles are no exception. In fact, they seem disposed to a few eye conditions, including dry eye, cherry eye, cataracts, glaucoma, lens luxation, progressive retinal atrophy (PRA), central progressive retinal atrophy (CPRA), and distichiasis.

Dry Eye (Keratoconjunctivitis Sicca)

Dry eye is unfortunately a common condition in Beagles. Tears contain antibacterial proteins, salts, and sugars and provide lubrication and flush away irritation. They even contain oxygen to nourish the eye. (The outer portions of the eye have no blood supply.) Tears are made up of water, oil, and mucus and are secreted by two lacrimal or tear gland glands—one right above the eye and another in the third eyelid, the nictitating membrane. If your dog can't produce enough tears, the eyes can become irritated and red. In time, even the cornea will turn brown, and a gooey substance (composed of mucus and oil without the water) will be discharged from the eye. In the most severe cases, a dog can become blind.

Lots of things can cause dry eye, including distemper, a congenital lack of tear-producing gland tissue, exposure to sulfa-containing antibiotics, removal of the third eye and tear-producing gland, and most often, an immune-mediated destruction of the gland tissue.

The condition is diagnosed by the Schirmer Tear Test, which entails placing a filter paper over the eye and seeing how long it takes to become wet. Dry eye is treated with cyclosporine, an immunomodulating drug used in human organ transplant patients. It is applied as ointment or drops directly to the eye once or twice a day and works by suppressing the destruction of gland tissue. There is even a type of surgery available, but this is an expensive and delicate procedure performed only by veterinary ophthalmologists.

Cherry Eye

Beagles are prone to this condition, which usually appears during the first year of life. With this disease, the nictitating gland (third eyelid) protrudes into the medial canthus of the eye, becoming red and swollen. Basically, it looks as if there is a red berry stuck in the corner of the eye. Both hereditary and environmental factors may play a part in the development of this disease. The condition can be surgically corrected, although the gland itself should definitely not be removed, as that will cause dry eye.

Cataracts

Cataracts are unfortunately rather common in Beagles. While dogs can develop cataracts, just as humans can, there is new hope for their treatment, thanks to computer-aided technology that allows veterinarians to make a tiny incision in the dog's cornea. A small probe emits ultrasonic waves that break up the diseased lens, and a foldable synthetic replacement is then inserted. Old-fashioned cataract surgery required two incisions: one to remove the lens and another to insert the replacement. The new procedure decreases inflammation, pain, and complications and has a success rate of over 90 percent.

Glaucoma and Lens Luxation

Glaucoma is a condition of increased pressure inside the globe of the eye. Beagles seem most affected by primary open-angle glaucoma, usually appearing between two and five years of age. This is a hereditary condition caused by a recessive gene.

Lens luxation takes place in the later stages of glaucoma but may sometimes occur as a primary condition in Beagles. Without treatment, the pressure damages the eye, causing pain and often blindness.

Progressive Retinal Atrophy (PRA)

This condition refers to the degeneration of the retinal vision cells that eventually results in blindness. The retina, located inside the back of the eye, contains special photoreceptor cells (rods and cones) that absorb the light focused on them by the eye's lens. They convert the light into electrical nerve signals that are passed by the optic nerve to the brain, where they are perceived as vision. PRA usually affects the rods, which are used for night vision, first, and then the cones, which perceive color. In people, this disease is called retinitis pigmentosa.

The age of onset for PRA varies. It was first reported in Gordon Setters in Europe in the early years of the twentieth century, but since then, PRA has been recognized in most purebred dogs, including Beagles. The diagnosis of PRA is normally made by ophthalmoscopic examination and requires dilatation of the dog's pupil through the application of eye drops. Confirmation of the diagnosis can be undertaken by electroretinography, an electrical measurement of retinal function. Unfortunately, there is no cure or treatment for the disease.

Central Progressive Retinal Atrophy (CPRA)

This disease is characterized by a degeneration of the retinal pigment and also of the rods and cones that absorb the light focused on them by the eye's lens. Most dogs lose central vision, although peripheral vision may last until old age. It occurs mostly in dogs under two years of age and is hereditary. There is no cure or treatment for CPRA.

Distichiasis

Distichiasis is a condition in which the eyelashes grow on the wrong place on the margin of the eye, causing irritation. It appears in dogs under one year of age and is hereditary. In a related condition called ectopic cilia, the eyelashes grow on the inner surface of the eyelid. The condition is congenital and hereditary. To treat distichiasis, surgery involving removal of the follicles is sometimes recommended.

Kidney (Renal) Disease

Many causes of kidney disease exist. Usually, renal problems are divided into sudden (acute) or long term (chronic). Acute kidney problems are brought on by blood loss, shock, trauma, poisons, infection, or obstructed urine flow. Chronic kidney disease may be rooted in heredity, immune system problems, or nutritional factors. Beagles in particular can be vulnerable to unilateral agenesis (uncommon, but with a high prevalence reported in certain lines), renal dysplasia, and polycystic kidneys. Most of these diseases occur in older Beagles.

Unfortunately, most signs of kidney disease do not appear until two-thirds of the function of the kidney is lost, and once chronic kidney failure develops, it cannot be reversed. However, feeding a vet-prescribed food designed especially to assist in the management of the disease can slow its progression.

Bladder Stones

The technical name for this condition is urolithiasis, and it refers to the occurrence of "stones" in the urinary tract. These usually occur in the bladder itself, although they can also be present in the kidneys, ureters, (tubes that carry urine from the kidneys to the bladder), or urethra.

Signs of bladder stones include bloody urine, frequent urination, passing only a small amount of urine, and straining to urinate. However, some severely affected animals show no outward signs at all, although the stones may show up on an x-ray as white circles. Just because a dog doesn't show outward symptoms doesn't mean the condition isn't dangerous, though. If a stone gets caught in the ureters or urethra, it can obstruct urine flow completely, which leads to a painful death. If this happens, only emergency surgery can save the animal.

Bladder stones come in several different varieties, and all of them develop in the same way, as minerals that exist in the urine as individual microscopic crystals. Over time, these crystals collect into grains that slowly build into stones that can reach 3 or 4 inches in diameter. No one knows why some dogs get bladder stones, but possible factors include genetic predisposition, bacterial infections, diet, and urine pH, probably in some sort of combination.

Treatment can be medical, surgical, or a combination of the two. The surgical procedure (cystotomy) is a fairly simple one, and the dog can go home the next day. In some cases, medical treatment alone will do the trick. For certain kinds of bladder stones, your vet may prescribe medications that acidify the urine. She may also prescribe a special diet, in which case she will advise you not to use a urine acidifier at the same time.

Urination Problems

Frequent urination can indicate kidney trouble, bladder or urinary tract infections, crystals, diabetes, and a host of other things. Get a sample if you can to take to the vet.

Straining to urinate is very serious. This could indicate an infection, a blockage, or prostate trouble. Don't try to guess, though; it's important to take your Beagle to the vet immediately if you notice your dog is straining to urinate.

If your older dog suddenly begins urinating in the home, you may need the services of your veterinarian. The first thing you'll need to do is to figure out whether the house soiling is medical or behavioral. When an adult dog can't "hold it," it's called incontinence. Dogs with incontinence often have a secondary irritation in the genital

If Your Beagle Needs Surgery

All surgery, even routine surgery like neutering and dental work, can be risky. Not only is there always a chance of a reaction to anesthesia, but surgery might also uncover an underlying problem—under not-so-ideal circumstances. Your vet may suggest that bloodwork be performed before surgery to check for abnormalities in kidney or liver function. If there is a problem with these organs, though, the dog may not be able to handle the anesthesia, as many drugs used for anesthesia are metabolized by the liver and excreted by the kidneys in the urine. Checking for these problems in advance could save your dog's life. This is why if your vet suggests presurgical bloodwork, you may want to consider having it done. It will cost a little more, but your Beagle is worth it.

If your Beagle does have a problem with his liver or kidneys, he can still undergo surgery. However, the surgeon will need to select a different anesthesia.

Several kidney conditions may cause your Beagle difficulty in urinating.

area, which they may lick excessively. If you suspect incontinence, take your dog to the vet for a checkup. Several drugs are available to help.

Liver Disease

The liver is a critical organ in the body, and it can be damaged by several factors, including viral and bacterial infections, toxins, and altered blood flow to the liver due to heart disease or other inherited abnormalities. Any liver disease is very serious, and the following are common in Beagles.

Hepatitis

Hepatitis is just a fancy term for inflammation of the liver, the largest internal organ. The liver performs many functions, but the most important is to cleanse the body of toxins. Hepatitis is an insidious condition that can destroy most of the liver, replacing it with scar tissue before you even know your dog is sick. (About 75 percent of the liver can be destroyed before you know something is wrong.) It has many causes, but chief among them are the canine adenovirus-1 pathogen, leptospirosis, and drugs like acetaminophen. Signs of hepatitis include depression, fever, lack of appetite, vomiting, diarrhea, jaundice, and abdominal discomfort.

If the cause of hepatitis is something simple or relatively benign, then it can be cured. More serious cases can be treated or sent into remission. If your dog has chronic hepatitis, your vet may prescribe a low-protein diet and lactulose, a medication that keeps the bowels moving rapidly and maintains low levels of ammonia in the blood. (High ammonia levels lead to confusion and other neurological problems.) Your vet may also wish to supplement SAM-e, an antioxidant that helps protect the liver.

Lumps and Bumps

Beagles are prone to many conditions that produce lumps. A sudden lump doesn't mean he's about to die, but it may warrant a trip to the vet, especially if this is your first experience with dog lumps. As your Beagle ages, he is more likely to acquire various bumps, warts, cysts, and tumors. While most tumors are benign (not spreading to other organs), a cursory glance can't differentiate between a benign cyst and a dangerous tumor. In addition, many benign tumors must be removed because they can cause problems with surrounding tissues; they can also erupt and cause infection. If you do find a mass on your dog, ask your vet to check it out. Vets have various methods to diagnose lumps, including impression smears, needle biopsies, CT scans, and x-ray evaluations.

Nervous System Disorders

The nervous system is the headquarters of your dog's behavior and movement, so it is crucial that everything functions properly in this area.

Canine Cognitive Dysfunction (CCD)

According to Pfizer Pharmaceutical, 62 percent of dogs aged ten years and older may develop signs of canine cognitive dysfunction (CCD). While not identical to Alzheimer's disease, the changes in the brains of dogs with CCD are similar to those with Alzheimer's. No one knows why these changes in the brain occur. Genetics may play a role, but environmental factors might also be important. Some people suggest excessive vaccination or stress could be responsible. Signs include:

- Confusion or disorientation. (The dog may get lost in his own back yard or become trapped in corners or behind furniture.)
- Forgetting housetraining.
- Maintaining lower levels of activity.
- Not recognizing people or other pets.
- Pacing, lying awake all night, or changes in sleeping patterns.
- Staring vaguely into space.

Luckily, there is a special medication available that can successfully manage this condition. Talk to your vet to discuss your options.

Epilepsy

Epilepsy is a disorder characterized by recurring seizures that occur when the neurons in the brain don't fire as they should. No one knows why this occurs, although one guess is that the neurotransmitters in the brain are not in proper chemical balance. Sometimes the cause of the seizure is known; for example, congenital defects, high or low blood glucose levels, low oxygen levels in the blood, kidney or liver disorders, infections, brain tumors, and toxins can all produce convulsions. (This is referred to as symptomatic or secondary epilepsy.) Sometimes, though, the cause is never discovered. When this happens, the disease is termed idiopathic or primary epilepsy. It most commonly appears in animals two to three years of age, and Beagles are one of the breeds most commonly affected.

The most common kind of seizure is a grand mal seizure, one in which the dog falls to his side or scrambles around on the floor. There is uncontrollable kicking or paddling, and the dog may defecate, urinate, or drool excessively. He is unaware of you or his surroundings. If the dog has more grand mal episodes without recovering from the first one, this is called status epilepticus, a condition which can be life threatening. If that happens, an emergency trip to the vet and intravenous drugs are needed immediately.

Most epileptic episodes have three phases:

- **Pre-Ictal Phase** (**Aura**): The dog seems restless, attention-seeking, nervous, confused, or frightened. This occurs minutes before the actual seizure.
- **Ictus:** This is the seizure itself. There is not anything you can do to stop the seizure; just move things out of the way, turn the lights down, and speak quietly to the dog. Keep him warm if you can. Most seizures last only a minute or so, although longer ones are more serious. Do not attempt to put your hand in the dog's mouth, as you may be accidentally bitten. Don't worry—he won't swallow his tongue!
- **Post-Ictal Phase:** This phase occurs after the seizure. Again, your pet may seem confused and disoriented. A few dogs seem to experience temporary blindness. This phase may last for minutes or even days.

Idiopathic epilepsy cannot be cured, although it can be treated with oral medications. (Epilepsy can be cured if it is due to a treatable problem, like lead toxicosis.) Sometimes the dog will continue to have seizures, although they will be

One kind of common mass that older dogs get is called a lipoma, or fatty tumor. It is benign and usually does not need to be removed unless it grows very large and impinges on neighboring structures. If the lump is cancerous (malignant), your vet can treat it with surgery, radiation, chemotherapy, or a combination of these methods.

less frequent, shorter, and less severe with the drugs. Your veterinarian has a choice of several medications, although the perfect drug has not yet been discovered. Some drugs are used in combination.

CANINE EMERGENCIES

An emergency is a situation in which you need to get your dog to the vet as quickly as possible. Of course, not every ailment needs professional treatment, and even professional treatment can sometimes be scheduled somewhat at your leisure. However, the following symptoms require immediate action:

- Bleeding from the nose or mouth
- Broken bones
- Bloated abdomen
- Pale gums
- Diarrhea lasting more than 18 hours
- Muscle tremors
- Problems with breathing or swallowing
- Refusal to eat for 48 hours
- Repeated vomiting
- Seizures or disorientation
- Spurting blood (arterial bleeding)
- Unusual swellings, especially sudden, hard, or fast-growing ones

Bites and Stings

Creepy-crawlies are everywhere, and your curious Beagle is more than likely to have a run-in with a bee, hornet, wasp, centipede, spider, or scorpion sooner or later.

Most insect stings leave a painful swelling around the site. If the stinger is still in place, scrape it away with a credit card, or gently remove it with tweezers. To relieve pain and itching, make a paste of baking soda and water to apply to the area, or use a commercial product. A cold compress may also help. (You can even use a bag of frozen peas!) Bee stings in the mouth can be treated by giving your dog ice chips to chew to cool the area. You can also try to flush the area with a mixture of 1 teaspoon of baking soda and enough water to make a thin paste (using a turkey baster), but don't let him inhale the stuff.

If a poisonous spider has bitten your dog, he'll need veterinary care. Apply an ice pack or cold compress to the area to slow the spread of venom, and get him to the vet right away. Untreated dogs can go into shock and die. You should also immediately transport your dog to the vet if he shows signs of an allergic reaction, such as hives or difficulty breathing.

Bleeding

If your Beagle is bleeding, your job is to apply pressure to staunch it. Use towels or clean rags, and keep pressing until the bleeding stops. Resist the urge to pull off the cloth—you'll just remove the scab that is forming.

Much more serious than regular cuts, of course, are cuts that slice across arteries. Arterial

If your curious Beagle has a run-in with a stinging insect, gently remove the stinger and apply a paste to relieve pain and itching.

blood is usually very bright red and comes in spurts, rather than the steady flow of darker blood characteristic of surface or venous cuts. In case of arterial bleeding, you must stop the blood flow at once. Apply strong pressure to the blood flow. If the bleeding continues, apply pressure to the pressure point closest to the wound, between the wound and the heart. Pressure points are located in "armpits," the groin, and just below the base on the underside of the tail. Press firmly until the bleeding slows. You will have to relax the pressure for a few seconds every few minutes so that you don't cause tissue and nerve death. If there is a lot of blood, take your dog to the vet immediately.

Frostbite

Frostbite refers to tissues damaged by bitter temperatures and is most likely to occur when animals are wet, unsheltered from the wind, or ill. The parts of the body most likely to be frostbitten are the ears, tail, or toes. At first, frostbitten areas may seem normal, but within a day or so, the damaged tissue will swell and become painful. Within a week, the affected tissue will dry up and turn black, eventually falling off. The dying tissue can be attacked by bacteria, leading to a dangerous infection.

If you suspect frostbite, thaw the frozen tissues with warm (103°F to 105°F) water. Don't rub the area—you'll

Your Basic Canine First-Aid Kit

A first-aid kit can save your dog's life. And even if the problem you are treating is not life-threatening, it just makes sense to have all the items you need in one place where you or your dog sitter can find them easily. You can buy a prepackaged kit, or you can save money and assemble one for yourself. On the outside of the box, clearly label what it is, and write your vet's emergency phone number in big letters, as well as the number of a poison control center. Basic items should include:

- **Activated Charcoal:** For poisonings (1 gram per pound mixed with water).
- **Antihistamine tablets:** For insect stings and allergic reactions.
- **Betadine or Nolvasan:** For cleaning open wounds.
- **Blunt-nosed scissors:** To cut tape and clip hair. Keep these scissors with the kit, and don't take them out to use for anything else. You may not put them back, and when you need them, you'll wonder where they are.
- **Canine rectal thermometer:** For taking your dog's temperature.
- **Cortisone ointment:** Topical anti-inflammatory.
- **Cotton balls and swabs:** Various uses, such as cleaning wounds.
- **Eyedropper or dosage syringe:** To apply medication.
- **Eyewash:** To irrigate eyes.
- **First-aid cream:** To soothe and protect wounds.
- **Gloves:** Two pairs—one set of thin plastic gloves to avoid contamination, and heavy gloves if you fear being bitten.
- **Hand towel:** Cleaning up, drying hands, etc.
- **Hydrogen peroxide (3 percent):** Various uses, such as for inducing vomiting.
- **Ipecac or hydrogen peroxide:** To induce vomiting (1 teaspoon per 20 pounds).
- **Kaolin and pectin:** To help diarrhea (1 teaspoon per 10 pounds).
- **Magnifying glass:** To locate tiny objects.
- **Muzzle:** If you don't have one, you can make one from nylons or a strip of fabric.
- **Nail clippers:** In case of an accident to the nail bed.
- **Nonstick adhesive tape:** For taping bandages.
- **Nonstinging antiseptic spray or swabs:** For cleaning wounds.
- **Pepto-Bismol or Maalox:** Stomach coater for minor intestinal upset.
- **Petroleum jelly:** To accompany the rectal thermometer, also for constipation (1/2 teaspoon per 10 pounds).
- **Saline solution:** Various uses, such as irrigating wounds.
- **Stretch bandage:** For wounds.
- **Styptic pencil:** To stop minor bleeding.
- **Tweezers or hemostat:** To pull out splinters and other foreign objects.
- **Two rolls of 3-inch gauze bandages:** For wrapping wounds.
- **Vegetable oil:** For mild constipation (1 teaspoon per 5 pounds, mixed in with food).

only increase the damage. Call your vet for an appointment to have the damage assessed. (Dead tissue will have to be removed.)

Heatstroke

Dogs have very inefficient cooling systems. They don't sweat, and they are easily overheated. Heatstroke occurs when the normal body mechanisms can't keep the body's temperature in a safe range. A dog's normal body temperature is anywhere from 100°F to 102.5°F. A dog with moderate heat-stroke (body temperature from 104°F to 106°F) can recover within an hour if given prompt first aid and veterinary care. Severe heatstroke (body temperature over 106°F) can be deadly—*immediate* veterinary care is imperative.

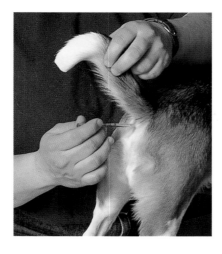

If your dog appears as though he is not feeling well, take his temperature to make sure he falls within normal ranges.

The following are the signs of heatstroke in the order that they usually occur:

- Rapid panting
- Bright red tongue
- Red or pale gums
- Thick, sticky saliva
- Depression
- Weakness
- Dizziness
- Vomiting (sometimes bloody)
- Diarrhea
- Shock
- Coma

If your Beagle has been affected by heatstroke, remove him immediately from the area. Even before getting him to the vet, attempt to lower his body temperature. Submerge his body in cool (not cold) water, or put in him in a cool or tepid shower. Cold water will shut down the capillaries and

Taking Your Beagle's Temperature

You can do this by yourself, but if you get someone to hold the dog while you take his temperature, things will be easier. First, apply petroleum jelly to the bulb of a rectal thermometer (one made specifically for dogs is best, but the baby kind will work, too). Slowly slide the thermometer about 1 inch into the dog's rectum. If you have an old-fashioned mercury thermometer, you'll have to wait about two minutes. Otherwise, just follow the directions. Next, remove the thermometer slowly, shake it down, and read it. A dog's normal body temperature ranges between 100.5°F (38.1°C) and 102.5°F (39.2°C). Temperatures below 99°F (37.2°C) and temperatures above 104°F (40°C) are considered extremely serious, and you should take your Beagle to the vet immediately.

trap the heat inside, something you definitely don't want to do. The cooling must take place gradually; if it occurs too fast, you'll bring on other life-threatening conditions. Check the rectal temperature every five minutes. When it reaches 103°F, you should stop the cooling process. Then, place him on a wet blanket and take him to your vet. Give him water or a children's rehydrating solution if the dog can drink on his own, but don't force him.

Your vet will give your dog more fluids, monitor him for shock, respiratory distress, heart abnormalities, and kidney failure. He may also take blood samples.

Dogs who suffer heatstroke once are at increased risk for a future incident. Prevention includes making sure your dog is never confined to a hot or even mildly warm car and providing him access to plenty of water and shade when he is outside. Overweight Beagles are more at risk, so keep your dog at his healthiest weight.

Inability to Breathe

Dogs who have stopped breathing may respond to cardiopulmonary resuscitation (CPR), and to be effective, it must be administered quickly. When performing CPR, you are giving your dog artificial respiration and chest compressions to get his heart going at the same time. If possible, it's best to have two people working: one for the breathing and one for the heart. Of course, that's not always possible. The chances of its success aren't great, but it is better than nothing. Also, no national standards for canine CPR exist, so guidelines vary.

A dog who needs CPR will be unconscious. You cannot perform CPR on a conscious dog. For one thing, it's ineffective and dangerous for the dog. For another, you'll be bitten.

CPR works using the ABC method: airway, breathing, and circulation.

"A" Is for Airway

If your dog is not breathing, the first thing you need to do is establish a clear airway.

Carefully pull the tongue out of the animal's mouth. Use gloves—a dog who is almost unconscious may bite instinctively. Bring the head in line with the neck, but don't pull if there is trauma to the neck area. Visually inspect to see if the airway is open. If you see a foreign body, put your finger in the back of the mouth above the tongue and sweep the object upward. If the object remains stuck, lift the dog upside down with his back to your chest, and give several sharp thrusts just below the dog's rib cage to expel it.

Close the mouth and do two rescue breaths (your mouth to his nose). If you are able to breathe into the nose with no obstructions, go to "B." If you encounter problems, reposition the neck and look down the throat for foreign bodies. If you see any, reach in and attempt to extract them. If that doesn't work, try the Heimlich maneuver: pick up the hind legs, holding your dog upside down, with his back against your chest. With your arms, give the dog five sharp thrusts to the abdomen to expel the object.

"B" Is for Breathing

Look and listen for signs of breathing. If there are none, place your hands around the dog's muzzle to prevent air from escaping through the side of the mouth, and breathe forcefully into the nostrils. The chest should *expand and fall* if you are getting air into the lungs. Rescue breathing should be given at a rate of eight to ten breaths per minute (or one breath every six seconds). Get your dog to the vet as soon as possible after he is breathing on his own.

"C" Is for Circulation

If there is no pulse, place the dog on a hard surface with his right side down. Use the heel of your hand to compress the chest on the lower side directly behind the elbow. The compression should be firm and not a sudden blow. It helps to have two people: the first gives the cardiac massage, while the second does the breathing. CPR should be given at a rate of 80 to 120 compressions per minute, with 2 ventilations being given every 15 compressions of the chest.

Poisoning

If you suspect your Beagle has been poisoned, check the label on the product if possible, and read what it has to say about toxicity. The treatment will vary depending on the poison and whether it has been ingested, inhaled, or absorbed through the skin. If there's a number on the package, call to get more details. Then, call your vet or poison control center right away. Be able to provide the name of the poison; how much was absorbed, ingested, or inhaled; how much time has passed since the event; how much your Beagle weighs; and the signs of poisoning your pet is displaying. If your Beagle is vomiting or has diarrhea, take samples to the vet to help with a diagnosis. Take the container that may have held the poisonous substance as well.

All poisonings should be treated as emergencies. If the exposure is to a topical poison, bathe the affected area in lukewarm running water with mild soap. If the poison is ingested, call your vet; you may be able to induce vomiting if the incident occurred less than two hours previously. (Don't induce vomiting if the dog has eaten a corrosive substance). You may also be able to give the dog some activated charcoal to delay absorption and bind the toxin.

CONVENTIONAL MEDICATION

If your vet prescribes a medication for your dog, don't leave the office without a clear understanding of what you're supposed to do with it. If there is something about the

If you think your pet has been poisoned, call your vet or the ASPCA National Animal Poison Control Center at (900) 443-0000 immediately. The charge is billed directly to the caller's phone. You can also call (888) 4ANI-HELP ((888) 426-4435), and a charge is billed to the caller's credit card only. Follow-up calls can be made for no additional charge by dialing (888) 299-2973.

medication you don't understand, ask the vet. Here is the minimum of what you need to know about each medication your pet receives:

- What it is. You should know both the generic and trade name of the medication.
- What illness or disease it is being used to treat.
- When to give it and for how long.
- How it should be administered.
- What side effects it may have.
- How it interacts with any other medications your dog is receiving.

Dispensing Medication

Undoubtedly you will end up giving your dog medication from time to time. Doing it correctly assures that you are giving the right medication at the right time in the right dosage. The obvious first step is to follow your vet's instructions to the letter—the directions on the package may also help.

When purchasing medication, you should know that as with human medicines, some kinds are available in generic form. These are almost always cheaper and usually of the same quality as the "name brand." Although both products must meet minimum standards, sometimes the name brand does provide better ingredients. Ask your veterinarian about each specific drug.

You should not order medications and immunizations through the mail and administer them to the dog yourself, even if you know how to give shots. You may save some money, but in the long run you'll be doing your dog a disservice. This is because when you take your dog to the vet, you are doing more than getting him a shot and going home; this is a chance to speak with your vet about your concerns and observations. It's also important for the veterinarian to see

Your veterinarian is most qualified to administer medication and immunizations.

your dog when he's healthy as well as when he's sick. This way, your vet can get a look at your "normal" Beagle!

Ear Medication

Ear medications come in many forms: liquids, ointments, and powders. Every package has specific directions for how to administer that particular medication, so follow them carefully

Eye Medication

To administer eye medication, stand behind the dog and place one hand on the side of his head to hold the head still and open the eye. Then, apply the medication with the other hand. Apply the required amount directly into the eye.

Pills

The trick to giving your dog pills is to do it so fast that the dog will be unaware he's been given a pill. In most cases, you can hide the pill in a bit of cheese, but if for some reason you can't do this, place your hand in the dog's mouth to open it, and insert the pill at the base of the tongue. Once the pill is inserted, close the mouth and hold for a few seconds. You can also blow in his nose. This will force him to swallow.

ALTERNATIVE AND COMPLEMENTARY MEDICINE

Contemporary pet owners (and their vets) are no longer limited to conventional treatments. New ideas in medicine are pouring in from all around the world. Some of the "new ideas," by the way, are thousands of years old, and many are quite effective. However, you should seek the advice of your veterinarian before attempting an alternative therapy.

Acupuncture

Acupuncture was first developed by the Chinese thousands of years ago. It works by stimulating the nerves and dealing with the patient as an "energetic being." Acupuncture uses inserted needles at various body points, most of which are located at the site of major nerve bundles and blood vessels. Inserting needles seems to activate the nerves, creating a cascading effect of increased circulation and the release of healing natural chemicals. It may be used in addition to conventional medicine. Acupuncture is often used to treat arthritis pain, kidney problems, and other chronic diseases. Treatment usually takes about 20 minutes and involves the insertion of 12 to 15 needles. Benefits last about two weeks.

Acupuncture should be performed only by a licensed veterinarian with at least 120 hours of study. A poorly trained person could puncture a blood vessel or do other damage. Just as with any medical treatment, acupuncture has risks, including a potential for site infection, although that is unusual since the needles used are small.

Chiropractic Therapy

A quarter of a century ago, nobody considered chiropractic treatment for animals, but as dogs are fellow vertebrates, there's no real reason why it shouldn't be used. Benefits of

Never give herbs to a pregnant or nursing dog unless your veterinarian approves.

chiropractic care include better circulation, mobility, and flexibility. It also reduces stress and has proven to be particularly beneficial for the canine athlete.

Herbal Medicine

As in human medication, herbal medicine and herbal supplements have become something of a trend in veterinary medicine. Herbs can be an effective method of healing. (After all, most medicines are ultimately derived from them!) They can be very effective in treating arthritis, cancer, seizures, stomach and intestinal problems, liver trouble, skin problems, urinary problems, and problems with the immune system. However, the correct use of herbs can be tricky; simply because they are natural doesn't mean they aren't powerful and sometimes dangerous.

In the first place, not all herbs are equal, and there are no codes currently in place to ensure a standard of quality. In addition, even if you know what herb to use, figuring out the dosage can be confusing—most of what you can buy in stores are dosed for a human being weighing 150 pounds. The best thing to do is talk with your veterinarian to see if he recommends a particular product.

Homeopathy

Homeopathy is a holistic system of medicine invented by Samuel Hahnemann, a German physician and chemist, about 200 years ago. Homeopathists believe that conventional medicine is too focused on signs and symptoms of disease rather than on the patient, who, they believe, often suffers due to a physical or emotional imbalance or instability.

Homeopathy is based on the old idea of "like cures like," and in fact the name homeopathy is derived from the Greek word "homios," which means "similar." Homeopathic medicines are natural substances (derived from plants or occasionally insects) prepared by a process of serial dilution (with water and alcohol) and succession, or repeated shaking. Homeopathists believe the shaking of the substance helps to conserve its energy and potency. The final product, which may contain extracts from more than one plant in pill or liquid form, has been diluted from ten times to millions of times.

In homeopathy, the more diluted the remedy, or medicine, the more potent it is believed to be. It seems counterintuitive that this should be so, but homeopathists swear by the results. Homeopathy does have the advantage of being inexpensive and free of side effects. It is most often used to help treat kidney and liver disease, arthritis, and hormonal imbalances.

Massage

The very touch of a loving hand is healing, and massage treatment turns a gentle form of relaxation into real therapy. Massage is an excellent treatment for older dogs, dogs with arthritis, and dogs recovering from surgery. It helps tone muscles and decrease soreness. Massage also helps reduce excess fluid around joints, stretch muscles, and increase mobility. It even helps remove metabolic waste products.

Massage may also release endorphins that ease pain. Not all conditions can be treated with massage, of course, and dogs with lymphoma or fractures can be made worse with this kind of treatment. If you begin a massage program, the first session should be very short—only five or ten minutes. If your dog yawns and closes his eyes during the massage, he is probably enjoying it, and you can continue a bit longer.

THE GERIATRIC BEAGLE

Your precious baby Beagle has become a dignified senior citizen. How did this happen? Well, it happened because you took great care of him and because Beagles are tough cookies. With continued excellent care, your Beagle can attain a great age!

Exercise

Older dogs need exercise just as much as younger ones do—they just need less strenuous work. When people stop exercising their dogs, they often stop the most important interaction between them, even if the owner thinks it's for the dog's own good. Something as simple as a daily walk will improve muscle tone and bone strength and solidify the bond between the two of you.

As your Beagle ages, continue to work with and exercise him. He wants to feel just as much a part of your life as ever. Healthy exercise is good for his mind, body, and spirit.

Diet

Your older dog has basically the same dietary requirements he did when he was younger—with one exception. Unless he has kidney disease, he needs about 50 percent more protein in his diet than he did as a young adult. Many senior dog foods now address this need. Older dogs are also prone to constipation. Adding fiber to the diet can help prevent or alleviate this problem. It will also make an overweight dog feel fuller when eating. Feeding a diet lower in phosphorus may also slow the progression of renal failure in older animals.

Senior dogs also benefit from additional levels of B-complex vitamins. This is because B vitamins help dogs handle stress, infections, and allergies, all of which are increased problems in older dogs. Older dogs may also require more vitamin E and possibly selenium and zinc.

Vaccines

Many people stop vaccinating their older dogs. They feel that the dog never goes anywhere anyhow, so why bother taking him to vet and exposing him to a procedure that may be risky? However, that may be the problem. Dogs who go out and about are more likely to build up immunities against wandering pathogens. Old dogs who stay home all day may have the poorest immune systems and the least resistance to such bugs when they do come along.

Saying Good-Bye

Dogs pass away, even the best of them. Especially the best of them, it seems. We all know this, but that doesn't make it any easier. It's never the right time for a dog to pass away, and nowadays, most dogs need our help. Typically, the dog becomes sicker and sicker, and although he's on medication, the good days get fewer and farther between.

Eventually, we make the heartbreaking appointment with the vet, or as happens more frequently nowadays, we ask the vet to come to us. Much has been written about the advantages and disadvantages of staying with your dog through the whole procedure, or waiting until he is asleep and then saying goodbye, or even leaving him in the hands of his old friend the vet. You alone know what's best for you

If you take good care of your Beagle while he's younger, he can attain a great age.

The Hospice Movement

Most of us are well aware of the good work hospice care does for human beings. It comforts both the living and dying and helps make the passage from life to the next world as easy as possible. The same care is actually available for dogs! Its goal is to provide a quiet, dignified dying process for both pet and owner. Some hospice care relies upon conventional painkillers, while others use a more holistic approach. All kinds attempt to alleviate pain and distress while allowing the dog to choose his own time to die.

and him. It is not true that the dog will necessarily suffer more if you don't stay. Some people simply can't handle the experience without falling to pieces before it even starts. Go with your heart, and don't feel guilty about your choice. Your Beagle will understand.

Afterward, you will grieve in your own way. Some people like to give their pets funerals and beautiful burial spots, while others remember them in different ways. Many vow never to have another dog as long as they live. Some call a breeder or a rescue the next day. Again, unerringly, you will make the right decision. And someday, perhaps tomorrow, perhaps years from now, a certain pair of soft brown eyes will meet your own—and you'll lose your heart all over again.

THE AMERICAN KENNEL CLUB BREED STANDARD

Head

The skull should be fairly long, slightly domed at occiput, with cranium broad and full. *Ears*—Ears set on moderately low, long, reaching when drawn out nearly, if not quite, to the end of the nose; fine in texture, fairly broad-with almost entire absence of erectile power-setting close to the head, with the forward edge slightly inturning to the cheek—rounded at tip. *Eyes*—Eyes large, set well apart-soft and hound-like—expression gentle and pleading; of a brown or hazel color. *Muzzle*—Muzzle of medium length-straight and square—cut—the stop moderately defined. *Jaws*—Level. Lips free from flews; nostrils large and open. *Defects*—A very flat skull, narrow across the top; excess of dome, eyes small, sharp and terrierlike, or prominent and protruding; muzzle long, snipy or cut away decidedly below the eyes, or very short. Roman-nosed, or upturned, giving a dish-face expression. Ears short, set on high or with a tendency to rise above the point of origin.

Neck and Throat—Neck rising free and light from the shoulders strong in substance yet not loaded, of medium length. The throat clean and free from folds of skin; a slight wrinkle below the angle of the jaw, however, may be allowable. *Defects*—A thick, short, cloddy neck carried on a line with the top of the shoulders. Throat showing dewlap and folds of skin to a degree termed "throatiness."

Shoulders and Chest

Shoulders sloping—clean, muscular, not heavy or loaded—conveying the idea of freedom of action with activity and strength. Chest deep and broad, but not broad enough to interfere with the free play of the shoulders. *Defects*—Straight, upright shoulders. Chest disproportionately wide or with lack of depth.

Back, Loin and Ribs

Back short, muscular and strong. Loin broad and slightly arched, and the ribs well sprung, giving abundance of lung room. *Defects*—Very long or swayed or roached back. Flat, narrow loin. Flat ribs.

Forelegs and Feet

Forelegs—Straight, with plenty of bone in proportion to size of the hound. Pasterns short and straight. *Feet*—Close, round and firm. Pad full and hard. *Defects*—Out at elbows. Knees knuckled over forward, or bent backward. Forelegs crooked or Dachshund-like. Feet long, open or spreading.

Hips, Thighs, Hind Legs and Feet

Hips and thighs strong and well muscled, giving abundance of propelling power. Stifles strong and well let down. Hocks firm, symmetrical and moderately bent. Feet close and firm. *Defects*—Cowhocks, or straight hocks. Lack of muscle and propelling power. Open feet.

Tail

Set moderately high; carried gaily, but not turned forward over the back; with slight curve; short as compared with size of the hound; with brush. *Defects*—A long tail. Teapot curve or inclined forward from the root. Rat tail with absence of brush.

Coat

A close, hard, hound coat of medium length. **Defects**—A short, thin coat, or of a soft quality.

Color

Any true hound color.

General Appearance

A miniature Foxhound, solid and big for his inches, with the wear-and-tear look of the hound that can last in the chase and follow his quarry to the death.

Varieties

There shall be two varieties:
Thirteen Inch—which shall be for hounds not exceeding 13 inches in height.
Fifteen Inch—which shall be for hounds over 13 but not exceeding 15 inches in height.

Disqualification

Any hound measuring more than 15 inches shall be disqualified.

Packs of Beagles

Score of Points for Judging

Hounds   General levelness of pack 40%   Individual merit of hounds <u>30%</u>   70%   Manners 20%   Appointments <u>10%</u> **Total** 100%

Levelness of Pack

The first thing in a pack to be considered is that they present a unified appearance. The hounds must be as near to the same height, weight, conformation and color as possible.

Individual Merit of the Hounds

Is the individual bench-show quality of the hounds. A very level and sporty pack can be gotten together and not a single hound be a good Beagle. This is to be avoided.

Manners

The hounds must all work gaily and cheerfully, with flags up—obeying all commands cheerfully. They should be broken to heel up, kennel up, follow promptly and stand. Cringing, sulking, lying down to be avoided. Also, a pack must not work as though in terror of master and whips. In Beagle packs it is recommended that the whip be used as little as possible.

Appointments

Master and whips should be dressed alike, the master or huntsman to carry horn—the whips and master to carry light thong whips. One whip should carry extra couplings on shoulder strap.

Recommendations for Show Livery

Black velvet cap, white stock, green coat, white breeches or knickerbockers, green or black stockings, white spats, black or dark brown shoes. Vest and gloves optional. Ladies should turn out exactly the same except for a white skirt instead of white breeches.

Approved September 10, 1957

THE KENNEL CLUB BREED STANDARD

General Appearance

A sturdy, compactly built hound, conveying the impression of quality without coarseness.

Characteristics

A merry hound whose essential function is to hunt, primarily hare, by following a scent. Bold, with great activity, stamina and determination. Alert, intelligent and of even temperament.

Temperament

Amiable and alert, showing no aggression or timidity.

Head and Skull

Fair length, powerful without being coarse, finer in the bitch, free from frown and wrinkle. Skull slightly domed, moderately wide, with slight peak. Stop well defined and dividing length, between occiput and tip of nose, as equally as possible. Muzzle not snipy, lips reasonably well flewed. Nose broad, preferably black, but less pigmentation permissible in lighter coloured hounds. Nostrils wide.

Eyes

Dark brown or hazel, fairly large, not deep set or prominent, set well apart with mild, appealing expression.

Ears
Long, with rounded tip, reaching nearly to end of nose when drawn out. Set on low, fine in texture and hanging gracefully close to cheeks.

Mouth
The jaws should be strong, with a perfect, regular and complete scissor bite, i.e. upper teeth closely overlapping lower teeth and set square to the jaws.

Neck
Sufficiently long to enable hound to come down easily to scent, slightly arched and showing little dewlap.

Forequarters
Shoulders well laid back, not loaded. Forelegs straight and upright well under the hound, good substance, and round in bone, not tapering off to feet. Pasterns short. Elbows firm, turning neither in nor out. Height to elbow about half height at withers.

Body
Topline straight and level. Chest let down to below elbow. Ribs well sprung and extending well back. Short in the couplings but well balanced. Loins powerful and supple, without excessive tuck-up.

Hindquarters
Muscular thighs. Stifles well bent. Hocks firm, well let down and parallel to each other.

Feet
Tight and firm. Well knuckled up and strongly padded. Not hare-footed. Nails short.

Tail
Sturdy, moderately long. Set on high, carried gaily but not curled over back or inclined forward from root. Well covered with hair, especially on underside.

Gait/Movement
Back level, firm with no indication of roll. Stride free, long-reaching in front and straight without high action; hindlegs showing drive. Should not move close behind nor paddle nor plait in front.

Coat
Short, dense and weatherproof.

Colour
Any recognised hound colour other than liver. Tip of stern white.

Size
Desirable minimum height at withers: 33 cms (13 ins). Desirable maximum height at withers: 40 cms (16 ins).

Faults
Any departure from the foregoing points should be considered a fault and the seriousness with which the fault should be regarded should be in exact proportion to its degree and its effect upon the health and welfare of the dog.

Note
Male animals should have two apparently normal testicles fully descended into the scrotum.

March 1994

CONVERSION CHART

US UNITS	MULTIPLIED BY	EQUALS METRIC UNITS
Length		
Inches	2.5400	Centimeters
Feet	0.3048	Meters
Yards	0.9144	Meters
Miles	1.6093	Kilometers
Area		
Square inches	6.4516	Square centimeters
Square feet	0.0929	Square meters
Square yards	0.8361	Square meters
Acres	0.4047	Hectares
Volume		
Cubic feet	0.0283	Cubic meters
Cubic yards	0.7646	Cubic meters
Gallons	3.7854	Liters
Weight		
Foot-pounds	1.3830	Newton-meters
Pounds	0.4536	Kilograms

Temperature

Fahrenheit to Celsius: Subtract 32 from the Fahrenheit temperature. Divide the answer by 9, then multiply by 5.

RESOURCES

ORGANIZATIONS

American Kennel Club (AKC)
5580 Centerview Drive
Raleigh, NC 27606
Telephone: (919) 233-9767
Fax: (919) 233-3627
E-mail: info@akc.org
www.akc.org

American Rabbit Hound Association (ARHA)
255 Indian Ridge Road
P.O. Box 331
Blaine, TN 37709
Telephone: (865) 932-9680
Fax: (865) 932-2572
E-mail: dmorga22@bellsouth.net
www.arha.com

Association of Pet Dog Trainers (APDT)
150 Executive Center Drive Box 35
Greenville, SC 29615
Telephone: (800) PET-DOGS
Fax: (864) 331-0767
www.apdt.com

Canadian Kennel Club (CKC)
89 Skyway Avenue, Suite 100
Etobicoke, Ontario M9W 6R4
Telephone: (416) 675-5511
Fax: (416) 675-6506
E-mail: information@ckc.ca
www.ckc.ca

Delta Society
875 124th Ave NE, suite 101
Bellevue, WA 98005
Telephone: (425) 226-7357
Fax: (425) 235-1076
E-mail: info@deltasociety.org
www.deltasociety.org

Dogs With Disabilities
1406 East Small Lane
Mount Prospect, IL 60056
Telephone: (847) 296-8277

National Beagle Club of America
1075 Route 82, Suite 10
Hopewell, NJ 12533
http://clubs.akc.org/NBC

National Dog Groomers Association of America
P.O. Box 101
Clark, PA 16113
Telephone: (724) 962-2711
E-mail: ndga@nationaldog-groomers.com
www.nationaldoggroomers.com

The Beagle Club (UK)
Secretary: Henry Haddy
www.thebeagleclub.co.uk

The Kennel Club (UK)
1 Clarges Street
London
W1J 8AB
Telephone: 0870 606 6750
Fax: 0207 518 1058
www.the-kennel-club.org.uk

Therapy Dogs International
88 Bartley Road
Flanders, New Jersey 07836
(973) 252-9800
E-mail: tdi@gti.net
www.tdi-dog.org

United Kennel Club (UKC)
100 E. Kilgore Road
Kalamazoo, MI 49002-5584
Telephone: (269) 343-9020
Fax: (269) 343-7037
E-mail: pbickell@ukcdogs.com
www.ukcdogs.com

Veterinary Pet Insurance
P.O. Box 2344
Brea, CA 92822-2344
Telephone: (800) USA-PETS
www.petinsurance.com

INTERNET RESOURCES

Beagles on the Web
(www.beagles-on-the-web.com)
This site offers an extensive list of international breeders, rescue organizations, and links on subjects specific to Beagles, including field trials and hunting, training, health, and rescue.

Beagle Rescue, Education, and Welfare
(www.brewbeagles.com)
This site is a great source of information about Beagle adoption and offers a thorough explanation on how to become a Beagle foster parent.

PUBLICATIONS
Books:

Fisher, Dave. *Rabbit Hunting.* Wrightsville: Woods N Water Inc, 2002.

Mason, Robert. *The Ultimate Beagle: The Natural Born Rabbit Dog.* Centreville: OTR Publications: 1997.

Serpell, James. *The Domestic Dog: Its Evolution, Behaviour and Interactions with People.* Cambridge: Cambridge University Press, 1995.

Magazines:

AKC Family Dog
American Kennel Club
260 Madison Avenue
New York, NY 10016
Telephone: (800) 490-5675
E-mail: familydog@akc.org
www.akc.org/pubs/familydog

AKC Gazette
American Kennel Club
260 Madison Avenue
New York, NY 10016
Telephone: (800) 533-7323
E-mail: gazette@akc.org
www.akc.org/pubs/gazette

Beagles Unlimited
Online Magazine
www.beaglesunlimited.com

Dog & Kennel
Pet Publishing, Inc.
7-L Dundas Circle
Greensboro, NC 27407
Telephone: (336) 292-4272
Fax: (336) 292-4272
E-mail: info@petpublishing.com
www.dogandkennel.com

Dog Fancy
Subscription Department
P.O. Box 53264
Boulder, CO 80322-3264
Telephone: (800) 365-4421
E-mail: barkback@dogfancy.com
www.dogfancy.com

Dogs Monthly
Ascot House
High Street, Ascot,
Berkshire SL5 7JG
United Kingdom
Telephone: 0870 730 8433
Fax: 0870 730 8431
E-mail: admin@rtc-associates.freeserve.co.uk
www.corsini.co.uk/dogsmonthly

Hounds and Hunting
P.O. Box 372
Bradford, PA 16701
Telephone: (814) 368-6154
E-mail: info@houndsandhunt-ing.com
www.houndsandhunting.com

ANIMAL WELFARE GROUPS AND RESCUE ORGANIZATIONS

American Humane Association (AHA)
63 Inverness Drive East
Englewood, CO 80112
Telephone: (303) 792-9900
Fax: 792-5333
www.americanhumane.org

American Society for the Prevention of Cruelty to Animals (ASPCA)
424 E. 92nd Street
New York, NY 10128-6804
Telephone: (212) 876-7700
www.aspca.org

Beagle Rescue Foundation of America
E-mail: info@brfoa.com
www.brfoa.com

National Rescue
Attn: Lynnie Bunten
11489 S. Foster Road
San Antonio, TX 78218
Telephone: (210) 633-2430
E-mail: kachina@texas.net

Royal Society for the Prevention of Cruelty to Animals (RSPCA)
Telephone: 0870 3335 999
Fax: 0870 7530 284
www.rspca.org.uk

The Humane Society of the United States (HSUS)
2100 L Street, NW
Washington DC 20037
Telephone: (202) 452-1100
www.hsus.org

World Animal Net (USA)
19 Chestnut Square
Boston, MA 02130
Telephone: (617) 524-3670
E-mail: info@worldanimal.net
www.worldanimal.net

World Animal Net (UK)
24 Barleyfields
Didcot, Oxon OX11 OBJ
Telephone: + 44 1235 210 775
E-mail: info@worldanimal.net
www.worldanimal.net

VETERINARY RESOURCES

American Academy of Veterinary Acupuncture (AAVA)
66 Morris Avenue, Suite 2A
Springfield, NJ 07081
Telephone: (973) 379-1100
E-mail: office@aava.org
www.aava.org

American Animal Hospital Association (AAHA)
P.O. Box 150899
Denver, CO 80215-0899
Telephone: (303) 986-2800
Fax: (303) 986-1700
E-mail: info@aahanet.org
www.aahanet.org

American College of Veterinary Ophthalmologists (ACVO)
P.O. Box 1311
Mediridan, Idaho 83680
Telephone: (208) 466-7624
E-mail: office@acvo.org
www.acvo.com

American Veterinary Chiropractic Association (AVCA)
442154 E 140 Rd.
Bluejacket, OK 74333
Telephone: (918) 784-2231
E-mail: amvetchiro@aol.com
www.animalchiropractic.org

American Veterinary Medical Association (AVMA)
1931 North Meacham Road –
Suite 100
Schaumburg, IL 60173
Telephone: (847) 925-8070
Fax: (847) 925-1329
E-mail: avmainfo@avma.org
www.avma.org

British Veterinary Association (BVA)
7 Mansfield Street
London
W1G 9NQ
Telephone: 020 7636 6541
Fax: 020 7436 2970
E-mail: bvahq@bva.co.uk
www.bva.co.uk

DEDICATION
To Stephanie, who loves Beagles.

PHOTO CREDITS